United States Government Accountability Office

Report to Congressional Requesters

August 2014

OIL AND GAS TRANSPORTATION

Department of Transportation Is Taking Actions to Address Rail Safety, but Additional Actions Are Needed to Improve Pipeline Safety

August 2014

OIL AND GAS TRANSPORTATION

Department of Transportation Is Taking Actions to Address Rail Safety, but Additional Actions Are Needed to Improve Pipeline Safety

GAO Highlights

Highlights of GAO-14-667, a report to congressional requesters

Why GAO Did This Study

Technology advancements such as horizontal drilling and hydraulic fracturing (pumping water, sand, and chemicals into wells to fracture underground rock formations and allow oil or gas to flow) have allowed companies to extract oil and gas from shale and other tight geological formations. As a result, oil and gas production has increased more than fivefold from 2007 through 2012. DOT oversees the safety of the U.S. transportation system.

GAO was asked to review oil and gas transportation infrastructure issues. This report examines (1) overall challenges that increased oil and gas production may pose for transportation infrastructure, (2) specific pipeline safety risks and how DOT is addressing them, and (3) specific rail safety risks and how DOT is addressing them. GAO analyzed federal transportation infrastructure and safety data generally from 2008 to 2012 or 2013 (as available), reviewed documents, and interviewed agency, industry, and safety stakeholders, as well as state and industry officials in states with large-scale shale oil and gas development.

What GAO Recommends

DOT should move forward with a proposed rulemaking to address safety risks—including emergency response planning—from newer gathering pipelines. DOT generally concurred with the recommendation and stated that it is developing a rulemaking to revise its pipeline safety regulations.

View GAO-14-667. For more information, contact Susan Fleming at (202) 512-2834 or flemings@gao.gov or Frank Rusco at (202) 512-3841 or ruscof@gao.gov.

What GAO Found

Increased oil and gas production presents challenges for transportation infrastructure because some of this increase is in areas with limited transportation linkages. For example, insufficient pipeline capacity to transport crude oil has resulted in the increased use of rail, truck, and barge to move oil to refineries, according to government and industry studies and publications GAO reviewed. These transportation limitations and related effects could pose environmental risks and have economic implications. For instance, natural gas produced as a byproduct of oil is burned—a process called flaring—by operators due, in part, to insufficient pipelines in production areas. In a 2012 report, GAO found that flaring poses a risk to air quality as it emits carbon dioxide, a greenhouse gas linked to climate change, and other air pollutants. In addition, flaring results in the loss of a valuable resource and royalty revenue.

Due to the increased oil and gas production, construction of larger, higher-pressure gathering pipelines (pipelines that transport products to processing facilities and other long-distance pipelines) has increased. However, these pipelines, if located in rural areas, are generally not subject to U.S. Department of Transportation (DOT) safety regulations that apply to other pipelines, including emergency response requirements. Historically, gathering pipelines were smaller and operated at lower pressure and thus posed less risk than long-distance pipelines. But the recent increase in their size and pressure raises safety concerns because they could affect a greater area in the event of an incident. In 2011, DOT began a regulatory proceeding to address the safety risks of gathering pipelines, but it has not proposed new regulations. Although states may regulate gathering pipelines, an association of state pipeline regulators' report on state pipeline oversight shows that most states do not currently regulate gathering pipelines in rural areas.

Crude oil carloads moved by rail in 2012 increased by 24 times over that moved in 2008. Such an increase raises specific concerns about testing and packaging of crude oil, use of unit trains (trains of about 80 to 120 crude oil cars), and emergency response preparedness. Crude oil shippers are required to identify their product's hazardous properties, including flammability, before packaging the oil in an authorized tank car. DOT has issued safety alerts on the importance of proper testing and packaging of crude oil. However, industry stakeholders said that DOT's guidance on this issue is vague and that clarity about the type and frequency of testing is needed. In July 2014, DOT proposed new regulations for crude oil shippers to develop a product-testing program subject to DOT's review. Additionally, unit trains, which can carry 3 million or more gallons of crude oil and travel to various locations through the country, are not covered under DOT's comprehensive emergency response planning requirements for transporting crude oil by rail because the requirements currently only apply to individual tank cars and not unit trains. This raises concerns about the adequacy of emergency response preparedness, especially in rural areas where there may be fewer resources to respond to a serious incident. Also in July 2014, DOT sought public comment on potential options for addressing this gap in emergency response planning requirements for transporting crude oil by rail.

United States Government Accountability Office

Contents

Abbreviations

AAR	Association of American Railroads
DOT	Department of Transportation
EIA	Energy Information Administration
FRA	Federal Railroad Administration
INGAA	Interstate Natural Gas Association of America
LNG	liquefied natural gas
Mcf	thousand cubic feet
MMBtu	million British thermal units
NOx	nitrogen oxides
NTSB	National Transportation Safety Board
PHMSA	Pipeline and Hazardous Materials Safety Administration
PSI	pounds per square inch
STB	Surface Transportation Board
Tcf	trillion cubic feet

August 21, 2014

The Honorable John D. Rockefeller, IV
Chairman
The Honorable John Thune
Ranking Member
Committee on Commerce, Science, and Transportation
United States Senate

The Honorable Ron Wyden
United States Senate

U.S. production of oil and gas resources has increased in recent years, driven in part by improvements in technologies. Oil and gas resources contained in underground shale formations were previously considered to be inaccessible because traditional techniques did not yield sufficient amounts for economically viable production. The application of horizontal drilling techniques and hydraulic fracturing—a process that injects a combination of water, sand, and chemical additives under high pressure to create and maintain fractures in underground rock formations that allow oil and natural gas to flow—have increased U.S. crude oil and natural gas production dramatically.

This rapid expansion of domestic oil and gas production has also changed dynamics for transporting these products to the market and has raised questions about safety. While pipelines transport the majority of oil and gas in the United States, recent development of crude oil in parts of the country underserved by pipeline has led shippers to use other modes, with rail seeing the largest percentage increase. Although pipeline operators and railroads have generally good safety records, the increased transportation of these flammable hazardous materials creates the potential for serious incidents. The explosion and fire caused by the July 2013 derailment of a crude oil train in Lac-Mégantic, Quebec killed 47 people and extensively damaged the city's downtown area, highlighting the consequences that may result from such incidents. The U.S. Department of Transportation (DOT) is responsible for ensuring the safety of the U.S. transportation system, including protecting people and the environment from the risks of transporting hazardous materials by pipeline, rail, and other modes. In particular, DOT's Pipeline and Hazardous Materials Safety Administration (PHMSA) has responsibility for pipeline safety oversight as well as hazardous materials transportation safety oversight for other transportation modes, including rail.

You requested that we examine the impact of shale oil and gas development on transportation infrastructure and safety. We are providing a broad overview of transportation infrastructure impacts and a closer look at the infrastructure changes and associated safety issues with pipeline and rail.[1] Specifically, this report addresses:

(1) challenges, if any, that increased domestic oil and gas production poses for U.S. transportation infrastructure and examples of associated risks and implications;

(2) how pipeline infrastructure has changed as a result of increased oil and gas production, the key related safety risks, and to what extent DOT has addressed these risks; and

(3) how rail infrastructure has changed as a result of increased oil production, the key related safety risks, and to what extent DOT has addressed these risks.

To identify challenges increased domestic oil and gas production poses for U.S. transportation infrastructure and the associated implications, we reviewed and synthesized information from studies and other publications from federal, state, and tribal government agencies; industry; academics; and other organizations. We identified these studies and publications by conducting a search of web-based databases and other resources containing general academic articles, government resources, and "gray literature."[2] We believe the studies and publications identified through our literature search provide key examples of transportation infrastructure limitations and associated implications. In addition, we analyzed data from the U.S. Department of Energy's Energy Information Administration (EIA) on oil and gas produced from 2007 to 2012. To assess the reliability of these data, we examined EIA's published methodology for collecting

---

[1]We focused our work on pipeline and rail because pipeline is the most used mode for transporting oil and gas products and rail has seen the largest percentage increase in use in recent years.

[2]"Gray literature" publications may include, but are not limited to, the following types of materials: reports (pre-prints, preliminary progress and advanced reports, technical reports, statistical reports, memorandums, state-of-the art reports, market research reports, etc.); theses; conference proceedings; technical specifications and standards; non-commercial translations; bibliographies; technical and commercial documentation; and official documents not published commercially (primarily government reports and documents).

this information and found the data sufficiently reliable for the purposes of this report.

To determine how pipeline infrastructure has changed as a result of increased oil and gas production, we analyzed PHMSA data on pipeline construction from January 1, 2010 through December 31, 2012 and interviewed DOT officials and industry representatives, including pipeline operators. To determine how rail infrastructure has changed, we analyzed the Surface Transportation Board's (STB) data for calendar years 2008 through 2012 on crude oil shipments by rail and interviewed DOT officials and industry representatives, including railroads. To identify the key safety risks related to changes in pipeline and rail infrastructure, we analyzed PHMSA data from January 1, 2008 through December 31, 2013 on pipeline and rail incidents, reviewed documents submitted as part of DOT's rulemaking on rail safety, and interviewed DOT officials and representatives from safety organizations, emergency responder associations, and industry. We assessed the reliability of PHMSA's data on pipeline construction and pipeline and rail incidents and STB's data on crude oil shipments by rail by reviewing documentation about the data sources, interviewing agency officials about how the data were collected, and reviewing related internal controls. We also reviewed some of the data for potential inconsistencies through testing and comparing the data to publicly available sources of similar information. We concluded that these data were sufficiently reliable for the purposes used in our report. Additionally, to examine infrastructure impacts and safety risks closely associated with transporting shale oil and gas, we interviewed officials and reviewed related documents from state oil and gas safety regulatory agencies, transportation departments, industry associations and oil and gas transportation companies (such as pipeline operators, railroads, and operators of rail loading terminals) in four states: North Dakota, Pennsylvania, Texas, and West Virginia. We selected these states because of their significant shale oil and gas development and varying geographic locations. To evaluate to what extent DOT has addressed safety risks, we reviewed federal laws and regulations and DOT emergency orders and guidance, interviewed DOT officials, and compared DOT's actions against risk-based management principles. See appendix I for a more detailed description of our objectives, scope, and methodology.

We conducted this performance audit from August 2013 to August 2014 in accordance with generally accepted government auditing standards. Those standards require that we plan and perform the audit to obtain sufficient, appropriate evidence to provide a reasonable basis for our findings and conclusions based on our audit objectives. We believe that the evidence obtained provides a reasonable basis for our findings and conclusions based on our audit objectives.

Background

Location of Oil and Gas Development in the United States

Oil and natural gas are found in a variety of geologic formations distributed across the country, such as shale and tight sandstone.[3] Shale plays—sets of discovered or undiscovered oil and natural gas accumulations or prospects that exhibit similar geological characteristics—are located within basins, which are large-scale geological depressions, often hundreds of miles across, that also may contain other oil and gas resources. Figure 1 shows the location of shale plays and basins in the contiguous 48 states.

---

[3]Shale is a sedimentary rock that is predominantly composed of consolidated clay-sized particles.

Figure 1: Shale Plays and Basins in the Contiguous 48 States

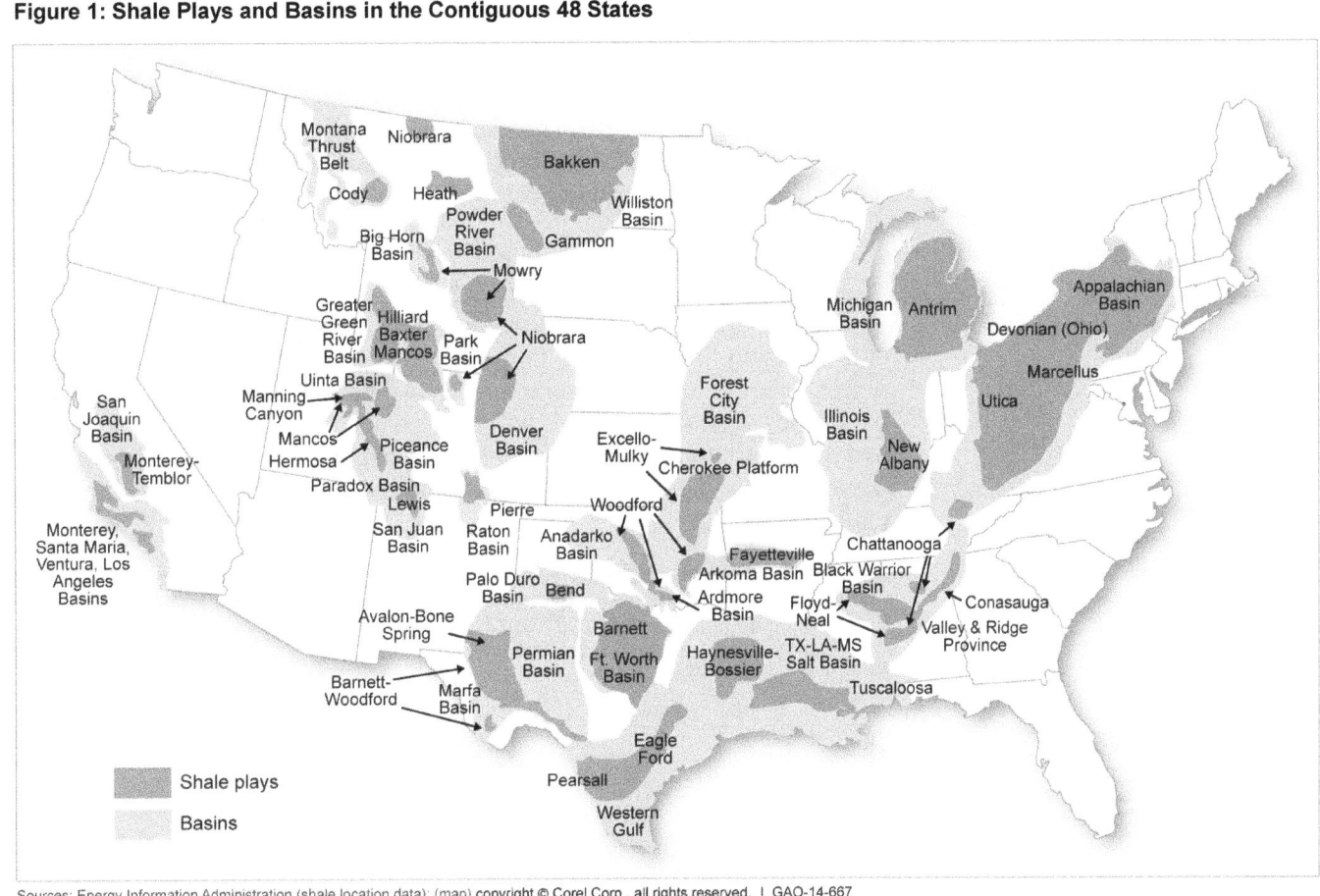

Note: Tight sandstone basins are found in some of the same basins as shale plays.

Shale plays can contain oil, natural gas, or both. In addition, a shale gas play may contain "dry" or "wet" natural gas. Dry natural gas is a mixture of hydrocarbon compounds that exists as a gas both underground in the reservoir and during production under standard temperature and pressure conditions. Wet natural gas contains natural gas liquids, or the portion of the hydrocarbon resource that exists as a gas when in natural underground reservoir conditions but that is liquid at surface conditions. The natural gas liquids are typically propane, butane, and ethane and are separated from the produced natural gas at the surface. Operators may then sell the natural gas liquids, which may give wet shale gas plays an economic advantage over dry gas plays. According to a 2014 EIA publication, operators moved away from the development of shale plays that are primarily dry gas in favor of developing plays with higher concentrations of crude oil and natural gas liquids such as the Eagle Ford in Texas, because given natural gas prices at that time, crude oil and natural gas liquids were more valuable products.[4] Another advantage of liquid petroleum and natural gas liquids is that they can be transported more easily through different modes of transportation than dry natural gas, which is transported almost entirely by pipelines to markets and consumers.

Oil and Gas Production

In recent years, domestic onshore production of oil and gas has been steadily rising. For example, from 2007 through 2012, annual production from shale and tight sandstone formations increased more than sixfold for oil and approximately fivefold for gas (see fig. 2). Horizontal drilling and hydraulic fracturing have advanced significantly over the last decade and are largely credited with spurring the boom in oil and gas production in the United States.

Figure 2: Increased Domestic Oil and Gas Production from Shale and Tight Sandstone Formations from 2007 to 2012

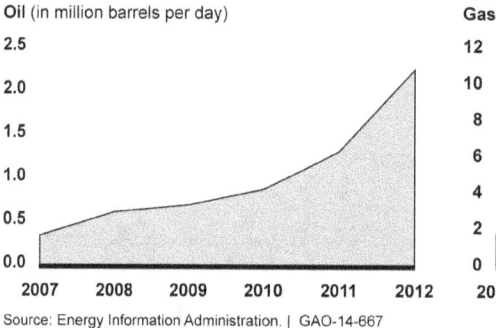

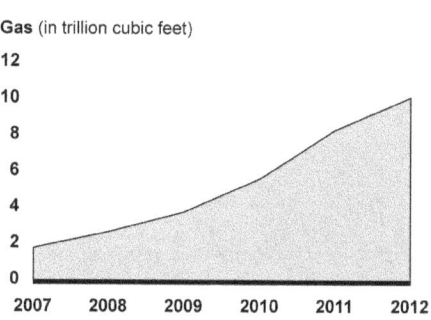

Source: Energy Information Administration. | GAO-14-667

Oil: Average domestic crude oil production from shale and tight sandstone formations in 2012 has increased more than sixfold compared with average production in 2007, from 0.34 million barrels per day in 2007 to 2.25 million barrels per day in 2012. To put this into context, according to EIA data, the United States consumed an average of more than 18

---

[4]EIA, "High value of liquids drives U.S. producers to target wet natural gas resources," *Today In Energy* (May 8, 2014).

million barrels of petroleum products per day in 2012.[5] According to EIA officials, oil from shale and tight sandstone formations accounts for 31 percent of total U.S. production. According to EIA, increased production in 2012 and 2013 was the largest annual increase since the beginning of U.S. commercial crude oil production in 1859. Much of the increase in crude oil production has been from shale formations, such as the Bakken in North Dakota, the Eagle Ford in Texas, and the Niobrara in Colorado. According to EIA officials, U.S. production of crude oil is expected to continue to increase—by 48 percent from 2012 to 2019—and will remain above the 2012 level through 2040.

Natural Gas: Domestic natural gas production in 2012 has increased about fivefold compared with production in 2007, from less than 2 trillion cubic feet in 2007 to more than 10 trillion cubic feet in 2012.[6] To put this into context, annual domestic consumption of natural gas was just over 25 trillion cubic feet in 2012, according to EIA data. In September 2012, we found that, assuming current consumption levels without consideration of a specific market price for future gas supplies, the amount of domestic technically recoverable shale gas could provide enough natural gas to supply the nation for the next 14 to 100 years.[7] Much of the increase in natural gas has been from shale formations, such as the Barnett, Fayetteville, Haynesville, and Marcellus formations.

---

[5]Petroleum includes crude oil and petroleum products. Petroleum products include gasoline, diesel fuel, heating oil, jet fuel, chemical feedstocks, asphalt, biofuels, and other products.

[6]Natural gas is generally priced and sold in thousand cubic feet (abbreviated Mcf, using the Roman numeral for 1,000). Units of a trillion cubic feet (Tcf) are often used to measure large quantities, as in resources or reserves in the ground, or annual national energy consumption. One Tcf is enough natural gas to heat 15 million homes for 1 year or fuel 12 million natural-gas-fired vehicles for 1 year.

[7]Technically recoverable gas resources are a subset of in-place resources that are producible given available technology. Technically recoverable resources include those that are economically producible and those that are not. Estimates of technically recoverable resources are dynamic, changing to reflect the potential of extraction technology and knowledge about the geology and composition of geologic formations. For additional information on shale oil and gas estimates and methodology to develop the estimates, see GAO, *Oil and Gas: Information on Shale Resources, Development, and Environmental and Public Health Risks*, GAO-12-732 (Washington, D.C.: Sept. 5, 2012).

Transportation Modes

Multiple modes of transportation, including pipeline, rail, highways, and waterways, connect oil and gas production infrastructure (such as wells and processing plants) in shale areas to customers, which include refineries, industrial users, and individual consumers. Additionally, when products switch modes of transportation, oil-loading terminals, sometimes referred to as "transload" terminals, transfer the product from one mode to another, such as when crude oil is transferred from a truck or gathering pipeline to a train. Responsibility for maintaining these modes vary: pipelines and rail are generally privately owned, while highways and waterways are generally public. Figure 3 illustrates how various transportation modes work together to bring oil and gas from production areas to users.

Figure 3: Oil and Gas Transportation from Production to Users

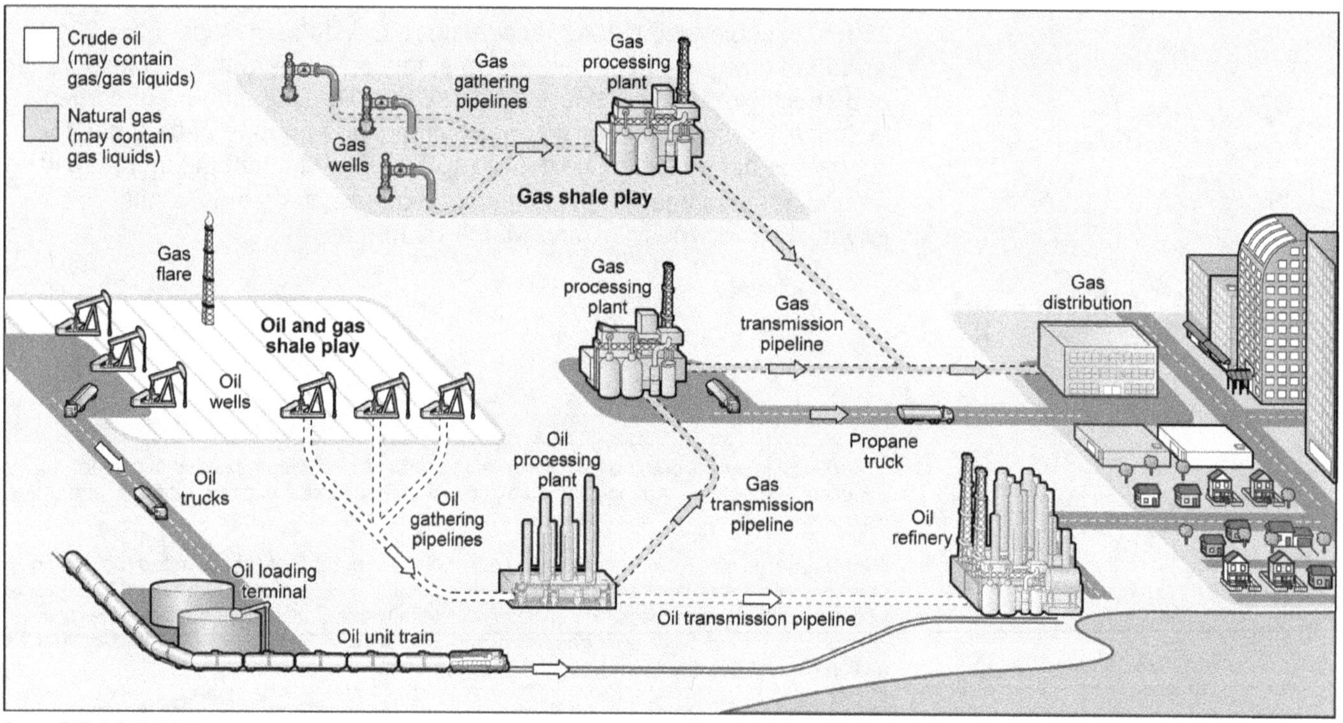

Source: GAO. | GAO-14-667

Note: This figure illustrates concepts presented in this report. It does not include all modes of transportation for oil and gas products nor does it depict all types of potential end users.

Approximately 2.5 million miles of pipelines transport roughly two-thirds of domestic energy supplies throughout the United States. These pipelines carry natural gas and hazardous liquids, including crude oil and natural gas liquids from production areas to end users, such as residences and businesses. Gathering pipelines collect produced oil and gas from their source and transport these products to processing facilities and transmission pipelines. Transmission pipelines then transport these products longer distances to users such as residences and businesses.[8] Distribution pipelines transport natural gas to consumers for use and are not within the scope of this report. Characteristics of gathering and transmission pipelines are described in table 1.

Table 1: Characteristics of U.S. Gathering and Transmission Pipelines

	Gathering pipelines	Transmission pipelines
Estimated number of miles	At least 230,000	More than 400,000
Function	Collect gas or hazardous liquids from production areas and then typically transport these products to processing facilities where they are refined.	Carry gas or hazardous liquid to communities and large-volume users (e.g., factories).
Description	Traditionally, range in diameter from 2 to 12 inches and operate at pressures ranging from 5 to 800 pounds per square inch (psi).	Traditionally over hundreds of miles long, range in diameter from 12 to 42 inches, and operate at pressures ranging from 400 to 1440 psi.

Source: GAO analysis of information from Pipeline and Hazardous Materials Safety Administration. | GAO-14-667

The U.S. rail network consists of about 200,000 miles of track, which runs mostly through rural areas. The railroad industry is dominated by the seven largest railroads, known as Class I railroads, which collectively accounted for more than 90 percent of annual railroad-freight revenues in 2012. Smaller regional and short-line railroads transport freight shorter distances and can help connect customers in areas not served by the larger railroads. The railroads' national association, the Association of American Railroads (AAR), represents the interests of the industry and works with railroads and other stakeholders to develop industry standards. Crude oil travels by rail in tank cars, commonly DOT-111 tank cars, which are generally owned by shippers or third parties. The DOT-111 is a DOT-specification tank car, meaning it must be built to conform to standards specified in DOT regulation.[9] It is a non-pressurized car that is used to transport a variety of liquid products, including hazardous,

---

[8]We use the term transmission pipeline to refer to both hazardous liquids and natural gas pipelines carrying product over long distances to users.

[9]See 49 C.F.R. §179.200. In addition to DOT specification tank cars, there are also tank cars built to specifications set by AAR.

flammable materials like crude oil. Terminals, referred to as transload facilities, transfer crude oil from other transportation modes (typically trucks or gathering pipelines) to tank cars for transport by train.

In addition to pipeline and rail, other modes, including barge and truck may transport oil and gas products. For example, barges may transport oil over longer distances on major waterways, such as the Mississippi River, while trucks typically transport oil over short distances to transload facilities. While this report provides a closer look at transportation infrastructure and safety impacts of shale oil and natural gas development on pipeline and rail nationwide, we also discuss highway infrastructure and safety impacts in the four selected states we examined (see app. II for a summary of highway-related impacts).

Department of Transportation

DOT is responsible for ensuring the safe transportation of people and goods through regulations, oversight, inspections, and other efforts, sometimes in partnership with states. Within DOT, PHMSA's Office of Pipeline Safety oversees the safety of pipelines through regulation and an inspection program, which includes over 100 PHMSA inspectors, and also collects information about the location of pipelines. PHMSA also has arrangements with states, which collectively have over 300 inspectors, to assist with overseeing interstate pipelines, intrastate pipelines, or both.[10] PHMSA's current pipeline regulations cover all hazardous liquid (including crude oil) and natural gas transmission pipelines. In addition to minimum safety standards that all transmission pipeline operators must meet, PHMSA employs a risk-based approach to transmission pipeline regulation and requires operators to systematically identify and mitigate risks in "high-consequence areas," which include populated and environmentally sensitive areas.[11] PHMSA also applies this risk-based approach to gathering pipelines and regulates gathering pipelines in non-

---

[10]These arrangements, in which states act as "agents" for PHMSA, can cover hazardous liquid pipelines only, gas pipelines only, or both (49 U.S.C. § 60105). States' pipeline safety offices are allowed to issue regulations supplementing or extending federal regulations for intrastate pipelines, but these state regulations must be at least as stringent as the minimum federal regulations (49 U.S.C. § 60104(c)). If a state wants to issue regulations that apply to pipelines that PHMSA does not regulate, such as federally unregulated gathering pipelines, there are no minimum federal standards that need to be adhered to, and the state is free to regulate as it sees fit.

[11]49 C.F.R. 192, Subpart O.

rural areas, resulting in regulation of approximately 10 percent of the nation's gathering pipelines.[12] Generally, PHMSA retains full responsibility for inspecting interstate pipelines for compliance with its regulations and taking enforcement actions when needed. However, states may be authorized to conduct inspections of interstate pipelines, as well as inspections and associated enforcement for intrastate pipelines. States can also promulgate regulations for intrastate pipelines, including gathering pipelines, even if these pipelines are not covered by PHMSA's federal safety requirements.[13]

PHMSA, through its Office of Hazardous Materials Safety, also regulates shippers and railroads transporting hazardous materials like crude oil by rail and other modes.[14] A memorandum of agreement details how PHMSA works with the other DOT modal agencies to address hazardous-material transportation safety. DOT's other modal administrations have responsibility for safety of their respective modes, such as the Federal Railroad Administration (FRA), which oversees rail safety. FRA enforces its own and PHMSA's safety regulations through inspections by FRA officials and state partners in some states.[15] PHMSA also has hazardous materials inspectors who enforce requirements for hazardous material packaging for transportation. Additionally, PHMSA's regulations include emergency response planning requirements for pipelines and the transportation of crude oil by rail. Specifically, regulations require operators of transmission pipelines and urban gathering pipelines to prepare emergency response plans and coordinate them with emergency responders.[16] Railroads that transport crude oil in tanks larger than 42,000 gallons are required to develop comprehensive oil-spill response plans with additional requirements for contingency planning, ensuring response resources by contract or other means, and training. Railroads

---

[12] 49 C.F.R. Part 192.5 and 49 C.F.R. § §195.1(a)((4) and 195.11(a)(2).

[13] For pipelines, there are 48 states, the District of Columbia, and Puerto Rico in PHMSA's natural gas pipeline program and 17 states in its hazardous liquid pipeline program (49 U.S.C. § 60104(c)).

[14] 49 C.F.R. Parts 171-179.

[15] FRA has 30 state partners for rail safety.

[16] 49 C.F.R. § § 192.615 (a)(8) and 195.402 (c)(12). Operators of hazardous liquid pipelines must also establish a response-training program and maintain firefighting equipment for their personnel who will execute the spill response plan, including firefighting equipment, techniques, and use of protective clothing.

are required to submit comprehensive plans to FRA for review. Otherwise, railroads are required to develop basic response plans, for which there are fewer requirements.[17] Because PHMSA applies a risk-based approach to its transportation oversight, we believe it is appropriate to apply principles of risk-based management to assessing the agency's efforts in this area. Risk-based management has several key characteristics that help to ensure safety, including (1) using information to identify and assess risks; (2) prioritizing risks so that resources may be allocated to address higher risks first; and (3) promoting the use of regulations, policies, and procedures to provide consistency in decision making.[18]

Increased Oil and Gas Production Presents Challenges for Transportation Infrastructure That Could Pose Environmental and Safety Risks and Have Economic Implications

Increased oil and gas production presents challenges for transportation infrastructure because some of the growth in production has been in areas with limited transportation linkages to processing facilities. According to studies and publications we reviewed, infrastructure limitations and related effects could pose environmental and safety risks and have economic implications, including lost revenue and hindered oil and gas production.

---

[17]49 C.F.R. § 130.31.

[18]We applied these principles to PHMSA's efforts in our previous report on pipeline safety, see GAO, *Gas Pipeline Safety: Guidance and More Information Needed before Using Risk-Based Reassessment Intervals*, GAO-13-577 (Washington, D.C.: June 27, 2013). A fourth principle, monitoring performance, was also discussed in that report.

Increased Domestic Oil and Gas Production Presents Challenges for Transportation Infrastructure

Though capital investments in U.S. infrastructure for oil and gas transportation, processing, and storage have increased significantly in recent years—by 60 percent from 2008 to 2012, according to a December 2013 industry report—expansions in infrastructure have not kept pace with increased domestic oil and gas production.[19] In the United States, most oil and nearly all natural gas are transported by pipeline.[20] According to EIA data, U.S. refinery receipts of domestic crude oil by pipeline increased almost 25 percent from 2008 to 2012, from 1.6 billion barrels to nearly 2 billion barrels.[21] However, according to a number of studies and publications we reviewed, including a 2013 report from the Fraser Institute, oil and natural gas production in the United States is outpacing the capacity to transport the resources through existing pipeline infrastructure.[22] In February 2013, EIA reported that pipeline capacity to deliver crude oil to a key hub increased by about 815,000 barrels per day from 2010 through 2013; however, the increase has been inadequate to transport crude oil from production sites to refineries. In March 2014, we found that most of the system of crude oil pipelines in the United States was constructed in the 1950s, 1960s, and 1970s to accommodate the needs of the refining sector and demand centers at that time. We also found that, according to Department of Energy officials, this infrastructure was designed primarily to move crude oil from the South to the North, but emerging crude oil production centers in Western Canada, Texas, and

---

[19]IHS Global Inc., *Oil and Natural Gas Transportation & Storage Infrastructure: Status, Trends, & Economic Benefits*, prepared for the American Petroleum Institute (Washington, D.C.: December 2013).

[20]In February 2013, we found that both the interstate and intrastate natural gas pipeline permitting processes are complex and can involve multiple federal, state, and local agencies, as well as public interest groups and citizens, and include multiple steps. According to some industry representatives we spoke with at that time, the interstate permitting process can be time-consuming, depending on the size and complexity of a project. GAO, *Pipeline Permitting: Interstate and Intrastate Natural Gas Permitting Processes Include Multiple Steps, and Time Frames Vary*, GAO-13-221 (Washington, D.C.: Feb. 15, 2013).

[21]According to EIA, a refinery is an installation that manufactures finished petroleum products from crude oil, unfinished oils, natural gas liquids, other hydrocarbons, and oxygenates. Oxygenates are additives, such as ethanol that increase the oxygen content of the fuel.

[22]For example, Fraser Institute, *Intermodal Safety in the Transport of Oil*, Studies in Energy Transportation (October 2013). The Fraser Institute is a public policy research and educational organization. For another example, see John R. Aures and John Mayes, "North American Production Boom Pushes Crude Blending," *Oil and Gas Journal* (May 6, 2013).

North Dakota have strained the existing pipeline infrastructure.[23] For example, according to a 2013 industry publication, oil production exceeded pipeline capacity in North Dakota by about 300,000 barrels of oil per day in the state.[24]

The limited pipeline capacity to transport crude oil has resulted in the increased use of other transportation options, in particular rail, truck, and barge (see fig. 4).

---

[23]GAO, *Petroleum Refining: Industry's Outlook Depends on Market Changes and Key Environmental Regulations*, GAO-14-249 (Washington, D.C.: Mar. 14, 2014).

[24]Kevin Smith, "Risk and Reward from the U.S. Fracking Boom," *International Railway Journal* (Sept. 11, 2013).

Figure 4: Crude Oil Refinery Receipts by Pipeline, Rail, Truck, and Barge from 2008 to 2012 (Millions of Barrels)

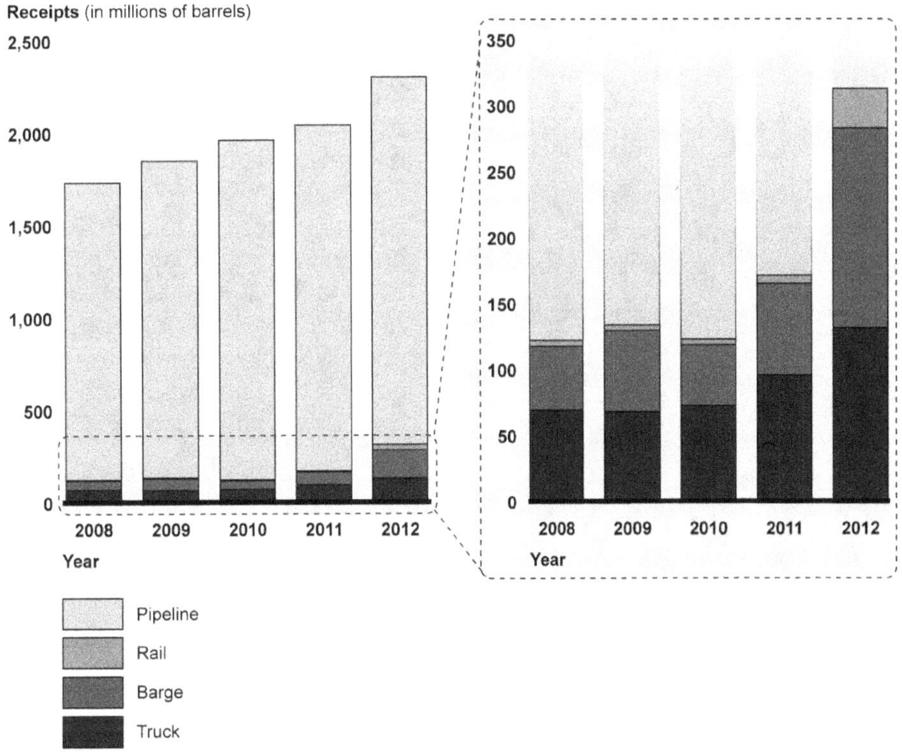

Source: GAO analysis of EIA data. | GAO-14-667

Note: Oil shipments may involve multiple modes. This figure indicates only the mode used for the last leg of the shipment.

- **_Rail:_** According to a 2014 EIA report, U.S. refinery receipts of domestic crude oil by rail increased more than sevenfold from 2008 to 2012, from 4 million barrels to 30 million barrels.[25] The increased use of rail for transporting crude oil is due to the increases in crude oil production in North Dakota, Texas, and other states, which have exceeded the capacity of existing pipelines to move oil from

---

[25]EIA, *Annual Refinery Report*, Form EIA-820 (June 25, 2014).

production areas to refineries, according to a number of studies and publications we reviewed.[26]

- **Truck:** According to a 2014 EIA report, U.S. refinery receipts of domestic crude oil by truck increased almost 90 percent from 2008 to 2012, from 69 million barrels to 131 million barrels.[27] In addition, according to a North Dakota Pipeline Authority publication, some natural gas liquids are transported to market by truck.[28]

- **Barge:** According to a 2014 EIA report, U.S. refinery receipts of domestic crude oil by barge increased more than 200 percent from 2008 to 2012, from 48 million barrels to 151 million barrels.[29] According to the EIA report, the increase in barge shipments may be partially explained by crude oil being transferred to barges from rail cars for the final leg of some journeys to refineries, particularly on the East Coast and along the Mississippi River.

According to a number of studies and publications that we reviewed, in addition to pipeline capacity limitations, rail, barges, and processing facilities and storage facilities also face limitations. For example, a 2013 industry publication identified a backlog for tank cars, needed to transport oil by rail, in the United States at nearly 60,000—representing over 20 percent of the existing U.S. tank car fleet.[30] In addition, a 2014

---

[26]For example, see Fraser Institute, *Intermodal Safety in the Transport of Oil*, Studies in Energy Transportation (October 2013); Paula Dittrick, "US shale production boosts midstream growth," *Oil and Gas Journal* (Nov. 25, 2013); and Statement of Adam Sieminski, Administrator, Energy Information Administrations, U.S. Department of Energy, before the Subcommittee on Energy and Power, Committee on Energy and Commerce, U.S. House of Representatives, 113th Cong., 2nd sess., March 6, 2014.

[27]EIA, *Annual Refinery Report* (2014).

[28]In addition to transporting oil to refineries, in 2012 we found that oil and gas development can require a few hundred to more than a thousand truck loads to transport the water, chemicals, sand, and other equipment needed for drilling and hydraulic fracturing. Further, some of the fracturing fluid that was injected into the well will return to the surface (commonly referred to as "flowback") along with water that occurs naturally in the oil- or gas-bearing formation, collectively referred to as produced water (GAO-12-732). The produced water may also be transported by truck from the well site to an injection well or a wastewater treatment plant.

[29]EIA, *Annual Refinery Report* (2014).

[30]IHS Global Inc., *Oil and Natural Gas Transportation and Storage Infrastructure: Status, Trends, and Economic Benefits* (December 2013).

Congressional Research Service report states that significant development of loading and unloading facilities could be required if rail is to continue substituting for pipeline capacity.[31] Further, a number of studies and publications identified that oil and gas production in some areas can exceed the capacity to process and store the resources.[32] For example, state officials in North Dakota reported in 2013 that maintaining sufficient natural gas processing capacity is a challenge of increased production.

Transportation Infrastructure Limitations and Related Effects Could Pose Environmental and Safety Risks and Have Economic Implications

A number of studies and publications we reviewed identified environmental and safety risks or economic implications from transportation infrastructure limitations. For example:

Risks to air quality: These risks can be the result of intentional flaring—a process of burning the gas developed along with oil—of associated natural gas that results from limited pipeline infrastructure and of engine exhaust from increased truck and rail traffic.

Oil and natural gas are often found together in the same reservoir. The natural gas produced from oil wells is generally classified as "associated-dissolved," meaning that it is associated with or dissolved in crude oil. In areas where the primary purpose of drilling is to produce oil, operators may flare associated natural gas because no local market exists for the gas and transporting to a market may not be economically feasible. In September 2012, we found that flaring poses a risk to air quality because it emits carbon dioxide—a greenhouse gas linked to climate change—and other air pollutants that can increase ground-level ozone levels and contribute to regional haze.[33] In January 2014, the North Dakota Industrial Commission reported that nearly 30 percent of all natural gas produced in the state is flared. According to a 2013 report from Ceres, flaring in North

---

[31]Congressional Research Service, *U.S. Rail Transportation of Crude Oil: Background and Issues for Congress*, R43390 (Washington, D.C.: Feb. 6, 2014).

[32]For example, Nick Snow, "Massive investment needed for oil, gas facilities, experts say," *Oil and Gas Journal* (May 28, 2012) and Ceres, *Flaring Up: North Dakota Natural Gas Flaring More Than Doubles in Two Years* (July 2013). Ceres is a nonprofit organization.

[33]GAO-12-732.

Dakota in 2012 resulted in greenhouse gas emissions equivalent to adding 1 million cars to the road.[34]

Increased truck and rail traffic associated with the movement of oil from well sites also creates a risk to air quality as engine exhaust, containing air pollutants such as nitrogen oxides and particulate matter that affect public health and the environment is released into the atmosphere.[35] Specifically, the Department of State reported in 2014 that increasing the number of unit trains transporting crude oil could increase greenhouse gases emitted directly from the combustion of diesel fuel in trains[36] and in 2011 we found that trucking freight produces more air pollution than other transportation modes.[37] Air quality may also be degraded as fleets of trucks traveling on newly graded or unpaved roads increase the amount of dust released into the air—which can contribute to the formation of regional haze.[38]

Inherent safety risks: Transporting oil and gas by any means—through pipelines, rail, truck, or barge—poses inherent safety risks. However, in January 2013, we found that pipelines are relatively safe when compared with other modes, such as rail and truck, for transporting hazardous goods because pipelines are mostly underground.[39] For example, we

---

[34]Ceres, *Flaring Up: North Dakota Natural Gas Flaring More Than Doubles in Two Years* (July 2013).

[35]Nitrogen oxides are regulated pollutants commonly known as NOx that, among other things, contribute to the formation of ozone and have been linked to respiratory illness, decreased lung function, and premature death. Particulate matter is a ubiquitous form of air pollution commonly referred to as soot. GAO, *Diesel Pollution: Fragmented Federal Programs That Reduce Mobile Source Emissions Could Be Improved*, GAO-12-261 (Washington, D.C.: Feb. 7, 2012).

[36]According to the Department of State's Final Environmental Impact Statement for the Keystone XL Pipeline, the use of liquefied natural gas (LNG) as a fuel source for trains is being developed and tested. The use of LNG could reduce greenhouse gas emissions compared to the use of diesel fuel.

[37]GAO, *Surface Freight Transportation: A Comparison of the Costs of Road, Rail, and Waterways Freight Shipments That Are Not Passed on to Consumers*, GAO-11-134 (Washington, D.C.: Jan. 26, 2011).

[38]T. Colborn, C. Kwiatkowski, K. Schultz, and M. Bachran, "Natural Gas Operations From a Public Health Perspective," *International Journal of Human & Ecological Risk Assessment* 17, no. 5 (2011).

[39]GAO, *Pipeline Safety: Better Data and Guidance Needed to Improve Pipeline Operator Incident Response*, GAO-13-168 (Washington, D.C.: Jan. 23, 2013).

found that large trucks and rail cars transporting hazardous materials, including crude oil and natural gas liquids, resulted in far more fatalities and incidents than pipelines. Specifically, we found that from 2007 to 2011, fatalities averaged about 14 per year for all pipeline incidents reported to PHMSA, including an average of about 2 fatalities per year resulting from incidents on hazardous liquid and natural gas transmission pipelines.[40] In comparison, in 2010, 3,675 fatalities resulted from incidents involving large trucks and 730 additional fatalities resulted from railroad incidents. Therefore, increased transport of oil and gas by rail, truck, or barge could increase safety risks.

According to state officials and several publications we reviewed, increased truck traffic resulting from increased oil and gas production can present hazardous driving conditions—particularly on roads not designed to handle heavy truck traffic.[41] Our analysis of data from PHMSA found that in recent years, the number of reported incidents involving the transport of crude oil by truck in both Texas and North Dakota has increased. Specifically, such incidents increased in Texas from 17 incidents in 2008 to 70 incidents in 2013, and in North Dakota they increased from 1 incident in 2008 to 16 incidents in 2013.

Barge accidents also pose safety risks and can have associated environmental and economic effects. For example, according to the U.S. Coast Guard Polluting Incident Compendium, in 2011, a barge struck a bridge on the Lower Mississippi River causing damage to the barge and a discharge of just over 11,000 gallons of oil.[42] In February 2014, a barge crash resulted in the spilling of about 31,500 gallons of crude oil into the Mississippi River, temporarily shutting down transportation along the river. According to a 2012 Congressional Research Service report, an oil spill from a barge can cause significant harm to marine ecosystems and

---

[40]More recently, we analyzed PHMSA's pipeline incident data for 2008 through 2013 and found that there was an average of about 3 fatalities per year from incidents involving natural gas pipelines and hazardous liquid pipelines that carry crude oil. Of the 17 reported fatalities during that time, 8 were attributed to a natural gas pipeline incident in 2010.

[41]For example, testimony of Dana "Sam" Buckles Tribal Executive Board Member Assiniboine and Sioux Tribes of the Fort Peck Reservation before the Senate Committee On Indian Affairs Oversight hearing on Tribal Transportation: Pathways to Infrastructure and Economic Development in Indian Country, 113th Cong., 2nd sess., March 13, 2014.

[42]U.S. Coast Guard, *Polluting Incident Compendium Part II* (December 2012).

individual aquatic organisms and negatively affect business activity near the spill, particularly businesses and individuals that count on the resources and reputation of the local environment.[43] For instance, the local fishing and tourist industry may be affected, and in some cases, a well-publicized oil spill can weaken local or regional industries near the spill site, regardless of the actual threat to human health created by the spill.

Economic implications: According to a number of studies and publications we reviewed, infrastructure limitations and related effects could have economic implications, including lost revenue, higher energy prices, and hindered development.

- ***Lost revenue:*** In addition to the risks to air quality from flaring, we found in October 2010 that flaring natural gas has economic implications,[44] and in April 2014 the Environmental Protection Agency reported that flaring results in the destruction of a valuable resource.[45] For example, in 2010 we found that on federal oil and gas leases, natural gas that is flared, instead of captured for sale, represents a loss of about $23 million annually in royalty revenue for the federal government. According to a 2013 report from the North Dakota Pipeline Authority, in August 2013, 2.7 percent of the total economic value and 7.2 percent of the total energy content being produced in North Dakota were lost due to flaring.[46] In another example, a Ceres report found that in May 2013 roughly $3.6 million of revenue was lost per day, at market rates, as a result of flaring in North Dakota.[47]

[43]Congressional Research Service, *Oil Spills in U.S. Coastal Waters: Background and Governance*, RL33705 (Washington, D.C.: Jan. 11, 2012).

[44]GAO, *Federal Oil and Gas Leases: Opportunities Exist to Capture Vented and Flared Natural Gas, Which Would Increase Royalty Payments and Reduce Greenhouse Gases*, GAO-11-34 (Washington, D.C.: Oct. 29, 2010).

[45]Environmental Protection Agency, *Oil and Natural Gas Sector Hydraulically Fractured Oil Well Completions and Associated Gas During Ongoing Production*, (April 2014).

[46]North Dakota Pipeline Authority, "North Dakota Natural Gas: A Detailed Look at Natural Gas Gathering," Oct. 21, 2013.

[47]Ceres, *Flaring Up: North Dakota Natural Gas Flaring More Than Doubles in Two Years* (July 2013).

- **Higher energy prices:** Growing shale development and the resulting increased availability and lower prices of natural gas have contributed to an increasing reliance on natural gas as a source of producing electricity in some parts of the country. However, pipeline infrastructure limitations have at times contributed to price spikes. For example, according to a paper from ICF International, pipeline limitations were a contributing factor to higher natural gas prices in the northeast in January 2014.[48] A cold weather pattern involving record low temperatures led to increased demand for natural gas for space heating and for generating electricity across parts of the country. With the surge in demand, several major pipeline systems became constrained and could not deliver sufficient natural gas to meet demand. According to a 2014 EIA publication, prices at the Algonquin, Massachusetts trading point, which normally are around $3 to $6 per million British thermal units (MMBtu) during unconstrained periods, reached up to $38/MMBtu in early January.[49] These price increases for natural gas led electricity systems to use more oil-fueled generating resources during this period.

- **Hindered oil and gas production:** A 2013 study sponsored in part by the Utah Department of Transportation found that oil and gas production from the Uinta Basin is likely to be constrained by limitations in the capacity of transportation infrastructure. Specifically, the study found that existing pipelines in the state are already at or near capacity, and by 2020, demand on the infrastructure network to transport oil and gas will exceed capacity—resulting in a loss of 12 percent of potential production over the next 30 years.[50] Further, according to a 2013 industry report, infrastructure constraints such as pipeline limitations and bottlenecks from the Permian Basin in Texas to a key hub have contributed to discounted prices for some domestic crude oils.[51] For example, we found in March 2014 that West Texas

---

[48]ICF International is a consulting firm that provides information to public- and private-sector clients.

[49]EIA, *Northeast and Mid-Atlantic power prices react to winter freeze and natural gas constraints* (Jan. 21, 2014).

[50]Duchesne County, Uintah County, Uintah Transportation Special Service District, and the Utah Department of Transportation, *Final Report: Uinta Basin Energy and Transportation Study,* Project No. S-LC47 (14) (Salt Lake City, Utah: April 2013).

[51]John R. Auers and John Mayes, "North American Production Boom Pushes Crude Blending," *Oil and Gas Journal* (May 6, 2013).

Intermediate crude oil—a domestic crude oil delivered to a key hub that is used as a benchmark for pricing for all crude oil—was priced just under $18 per barrel less in 2012 than Brent, an international benchmark crude oil from the European North Sea that has historically been about the same price as West Texas Intermediate.[52] These discounted prices mean resource developers have received lower prices for their crude oil production. According to a 2013 Energy Policy Research Foundation report, discounted prices may eventually lead to production growth constraints.[53]

DOT Has Not Fully Addressed Safety Risks from Expansion of Federally Unregulated Gathering Pipelines

Increases in the Number, Size, and Operating Pressure of Gathering Pipelines Pose Additional Risk, Particularly Where They Are Not Federally Regulated

Gathering pipeline construction has increased significantly as a result of increased shale oil and gas development; however, the increase in pipeline mileage is unknown because data on gathering pipelines are not systematically collected by PHMSA nor by every state. The Interstate Natural Gas Association of America (INGAA), a trade organization representing interstate natural gas transmission pipeline companies, estimated in March 2014 that shale oil and gas development will result in approximately 14,000 miles of new gas gathering pipelines and 7,800 miles of new oil gathering pipelines added each year from 2011 through 2035.[54] State officials in Pennsylvania, North Dakota, Texas, and West

---

[52]GAO, *Petroleum Refining: Industry's Outlook Depends on Market Changes and Key Environmental Regulations*, GAO-14-249 (Washington, D.C.: Mar. 14, 2014).

[53]Energy Policy Research Foundation, *Pipelines, Trains and Trucks: Moving Rising North American Oil Production to Market* (Washington, D.C.: Oct. 21, 2013). The Energy Policy Research Foundation Inc. is a not-for-profit organization that studies energy economics and policy issues.

[54]The INGAA Foundation Inc. *North American Midstream Infrastructure through 2035: Capitalizing on Our Energy Abundance, An INGAA Foundation Report, Prepared by ICF International* (Mar. 18, 2014), available at http://www.ingaa.org/File.aspx?id=21498 (accessed May 16, 2014).

Virginia said that companies have invested significantly in gathering pipeline infrastructure. For example, according to data published by Texas state officials, 15,684 new miles of federally unregulated gathering pipelines were added in the state between 2010 and 2013.[55] In response to the growth in gathering pipelines, Texas officials told us that their state enacted legislation to increase state regulatory authority over gathering pipelines. Similarly, North Dakota passed rule changes in 2013 to increase state regulatory authority over gathering pipelines. Texas officials told us that they plan to study and determine what parts of their rules should apply to gathering pipelines during 2014 and then issue guidance in 2015. In April 2014, North Dakota implemented regulations requiring companies to report the location and characteristics of gathering pipelines carrying any products including natural gas, crude oil, natural gas liquids, water, and others. The National Association of Pipeline Safety Representatives, an association representing state pipeline safety officials, produced a compendium of state pipeline regulations showing that most states with delegated authority from PHMSA to conduct intrastate inspections do not have expanded regulations that cover increased oversight of gathering pipelines.[56] As a result, companies building gathering pipelines in rural areas are generally not subject to inspection and do not have to report the location and characteristics of much of the gathering pipelines being installed.

Although the majority of the total gathering pipeline network that exists are the traditional small pipelines, state pipeline regulators, PHMSA officials, and pipeline operators we spoke with said that some newly built

---

[55]State officials from the other three states could not provide precise numbers on gathering pipeline construction because most of this new construction is in rural locations where pipeline operators are exempt from federal reporting and oversight regulations and these states, unlike Texas, did not have their own reporting requirements. PHMSA regulations for natural gas gathering pipelines do not apply to rural areas designated as Class 1 which is defined as any location with 10 or fewer buildings intended for human occupancy within 220 yards of the centerline of the pipeline for a 1-mile segment of pipeline, see 49 C.F.R. § § 192.5 and 192.8 . For hazardous liquid gathering pipelines, PHMSA regulates only certain rural gathering pipelines within one-quarter mile of environmentally sensitive areas, see 49 C.F.R. §195.11. However, as discussed in the background of this report, PHMSA regulates non-rural pipelines.

[56]Based on our analysis, we determined that expanded regulations vary by state, but the compendium shows that at least 6 states have some form of expanded regulation. National Association of Pipeline Safety Representatives, *Compendium of State Pipeline Safety Requirements & Initiatives Providing Increased Public Safety Levels compared to Code of Federal Regulations*, second edition (Sept. 9, 2013).

gathering pipelines have larger diameters and higher operating pressures that more closely resemble transmission pipelines than traditional gathering pipelines. For example, while gathering pipelines have traditionally been 2 to 12 inches in diameter, one company operating in the Texas Eagle Ford shale region showed us plans to build 30- and 36-inch natural gas gathering pipelines, which is near the high end of diameters for regulated transmission pipelines. Historically, federally unregulated gathering pipelines were low pressure, smaller-diameter pipelines and were generally in rural areas where there was less safety risk. Now, according to PHMSA, industry, and state pipeline safety officials we spoke to, gathering pipelines of larger diameter and higher pressure are being constructed, including in areas closer to populations. Such construction could increase safety risk, since an incident occurring on one of these larger, high-pressure unregulated gathering pipelines could affect a greater area and be as serious as an incident involving a regulated transmission pipeline of similar diameter and pressure.

Pipeline operators and industry organizations told us that new gathering pipelines are likely safer because new pipelines are less susceptible to issues like corrosion—a common reason for failure in older pipelines. Pipeline operators also told us that some large-diameter, high-pressure gathering pipelines are built to the same specifications as regulated transmission pipelines and that these pipelines are in very rural areas with little risk to people. They also expressed that safety is very important to the industry and that companies understand not only the potential harm to the network, people, and environment, but also the public perception following a high-profile incident and therefore manage their assets to avoid incidents. Nonetheless, state pipeline regulators, PHMSA officials, and safety organizations expressed concern with the potential safety threat of unregulated gathering pipelines of this size. For example, a citizens' shale development awareness group in Pennsylvania has documented construction of several unregulated gathering pipelines in the state that are 24 inches in diameter. The group argues that while these gathering pipelines are in rural areas, they are being built unnecessarily close to homes. PHMSA officials told us that the large diameter and pressure of the pipelines increase the concern for the safety of the environment and people nearby.

In addition to potential increased safety risk as a result of the changing characteristics of the pipelines, some stakeholders shared concerns about the readiness of emergency responders to address potential incidents that could occur with unregulated gathering pipelines. PHMSA's emergency response planning requirements that apply to other pipelines do not apply to rural unregulated gathering pipelines. Consequently, response planning in rural areas with unregulated gathering lines may be inadequate to address a major incident. Transmission pipeline operators with pipelines similar in size to the new gathering pipelines are required to develop comprehensive emergency response plans and coordinate with local emergency responders. Emergency response officials whom we spoke with stated that lacking information about the location of some gathering pipelines, responders—particularly in rural areas—may not be adequately prepared to respond to an incident. A representative from the National Association of State Fire Marshals told us that training and communication with pipeline companies are key for emergency responders' knowledge and awareness. Additionally, emergency response officials also told us that rural areas in particular lack the level of hazardous-materials response resources found in metropolitan areas where more is known about the extent of local pipeline networks. The National Transportation Safety Board (NTSB) has also stated that emergency response planning is critical for pipeline safety and has recommended that pipeline operators help ensure adequate emergency response by providing local jurisdictions and residents with key information on the pipelines in their areas.

DOT Has Not Proposed Regulatory Changes to Address Risks Posed by Gathering Pipelines

As previously discussed, PHMSA applies a risk-based approach to regulating pipeline safety. A key principle of risk-based management is promoting the use of regulations, policies, and procedures to provide consistency in decision-making. PHMSA has acknowledged the growing potential risk of federally unregulated gathering pipelines as more are constructed and at larger diameters and higher pressures, but DOT has not proposed regulatory changes to address this risk. In August 2011, PHMSA published an Advance Notice of Proposed Rulemaking, stating that the existing regulatory framework for natural gas gathering pipelines may no longer be appropriate due to recent developments in gas production.[57] In the notice, PHMSA asked for comment on whether it should consider establishing new, risk-based safety requirements for large-diameter, high-pressure gas gathering pipelines in rural locations, among other potential changes to gathering pipeline regulations.[58] The

---

[57]An Advance Notice of Proposed Rulemaking is an initial step in a rulemaking proceeding seeking comment on issues the agency may address in future proposed regulation.

[58]76 Fed. Reg. 53086 (Aug. 25, 2011).

proposal also states that enforcement of current requirements has been hampered by the conflicting and ambiguous language of the current regulation that can produce multiple classifications for the same pipeline system, which means that parts of a single pipeline system can be classified as rural gathering pipelines and therefore be unregulated, while other parts of the same pipeline with the same characteristics are regulated. PHMSA officials told us they have drafted proposed regulations for both gas and hazardous liquid gathering pipelines but as of June 2014, the agency had not issued the Notice of Proposed Rulemaking for comment. According to DOT officials, the proposed gas rule is being reviewed internally and the proposed hazardous liquid rule is with the Office of Management and Budget for review.[59] PHMSA officials also told us they have studied existing federal and state gathering pipeline regulation to help identify where gathering pipelines are currently regulated and remaining gaps; however, this study has been in the final stages of review during the course of our work and has not yet been published.

Given the lack of PHMSA regulation of rural gathering pipelines, the extent, location, and construction practices for rural gathering pipelines is largely unknown by federal, state, and local officials, and oversight to verify the construction and monitor operators' safety practices is lacking. In 2012, we concluded that unregulated gathering pipelines also pose risks due to construction quality, maintenance practices, and limited or unknown information on pipeline integrity. [60] We recommended at that time that PHMSA collect data on unregulated gathering pipelines to facilitate quantitatively assessing the safety risks posed by these pipelines, which we said could assist in determining the sufficiency of

---

[59]75 Fed. Reg. 63774 (Oct. 18, 2010).

[60]GAO, *Pipeline Safety: Collecting Data and Sharing Information on Federally Unregulated Gathering Pipelines Could Help Enhance Safety*, GAO-12-388 (Washington, D.C.: Mar. 22, 2012). For this report, we surveyed state pipeline agencies, among which there were 39 agencies that reported they had gathering pipelines in their state that PHMSA does not regulate. Eighteen of the state agencies reported that the quality of installation procedures and construction materials is a safety risk for unregulated gathering pipelines because the construction phase of pipeline installation is critical to ensure the long-term integrity of the pipeline. Sixteen state agencies reported that the extent to which pipeline operators maintain their pipelines is a moderate or high safety risk for unregulated gathering pipelines. According to agency officials, after a pipeline is installed and operational, periodic maintenance—such as inspecting and testing equipment—is important to prevent leaks and ruptures and could extend the operating life of a pipeline.

safety regulations for gathering pipelines. According to DOT officials, as of July 2014, PHMSA has compiled data on existing gathering pipeline requirements, and the resulting report is under internal review. Furthermore, officials said that data collection is part of the proposed rules also under review. In 2010, the National Association of Pipeline Safety Representatives recommended that PHMSA modify federal pipeline regulations to establish requirements for gathering pipelines in rural areas that are presently not regulated. The association stated that with the advent of new production technologies, there has been rapid development of gas production from shale formations such as the Barnett, Marcellus, and Bakken resulting in a significant amount of new gathering pipeline construction. Further, in these newer gas gathering systems, it is not uncommon to find rural gathering pipelines up to 30 inches in diameter and operating at 1480 psi, which is the higher end of traditional transmission operating pressure.[61] Enhanced pipeline safety for all types of pipeline was also on NTSB's "Most Wanted List" in 2013 and 2014. NTSB has prioritized overall pipeline safety because of the increased demand in oil and gas and the aging pipeline infrastructure.

Resources are an important consideration in evaluating how to address the increased risk of gathering pipelines. According to PHMSA officials, inspection resources are limited and would be further stretched if rural gathering pipelines were regulated. If PHMSA were to receive increased staff funding in the near future, there could be a lag in ramping up the inspection workforce because inspectors would have to complete PHMSA's 3-year pipeline-inspection training to become fully certified.[62] However, if PHMSA were to set minimum federal regulations for gathering pipelines, this would enable the agency to include currently federally unregulated rural gathering lines in decisions for prioritizing resources for addressing safety risks. This is in line with the principles of risk-based management, while also enabling data-driven, evidence-based decisions about the risks of rural gathering pipelines, which our previous

[61]National Association of Pipeline Safety Representatives, *Urging PHMSA to Establish Regulatory Requirements for Gas Gathering Lines in Class 1 Areas*, Resolution 2010-2 AC-2 (Sept. 30, 2010).

[62] Some state officials also expressed concern about the capacity of PHMSA's inspector training program, which all state inspectors are also required to complete. The 3-year program must be completed mostly in PHMSA's Oklahoma City, Oklahoma, training center, which can create scheduling and budget challenges.

work has shown is especially important in a time of limited resources.[63] State regulators in all four states we spoke with acknowledged their resources could also be strained; however, the officials supported regulating rural gathering pipelines. State officials said that without rural gathering pipeline regulation, such as provisions for inspections or industry reporting, they have limited knowledge of the construction and maintenance practices of rural gathering pipeline operators, do not always know where new rural gathering pipelines are being constructed, and may not even have communication with the operators.

Transmission Pipeline Infrastructure Has Not Increased Substantially as a Result of Shale Development

Gas flows from shale plays into transmission pipelines have increased, but construction of new transmission pipelines has not increased dramatically as a result of increased shale development. According to PHMSA data, approximately 4,500 miles of new oil and gas transmission pipelines were built between January 2010 and December 2012. This includes about 2,000 miles each of crude oil and natural gas pipelines and the remaining is pipeline for natural gas liquids.

Oil and gas pipeline industry representatives and transmission pipeline companies we spoke with stated that transmission pipeline companies have been able to accommodate increased demand in various ways. Transmission pipeline companies have repurposed existing pipelines, made operational changes—including increased compression and change in directional flow—and added additional capacity to the current network through smaller-scale construction projects. Companies have repurposed pipelines by changing them from one product to another, such as converting a natural gas pipeline to a natural gas liquid pipeline or a crude oil pipeline. Companies have also instituted operational changes such as adding additional compression to their line, which allows them to move more gas through the same lines, and changing directional flow of a pipeline. One pipeline operator we spoke with is reversing flow of its gas transmission pipeline. Prior to shale development, this pipeline moved natural gas from the Gulf Coast to the Northeast. By 2017, the volume of gas that once flowed north will flow south. The pipeline operator stated that changing the direction of the flow, while not as easy as flipping a switch, requires significantly less time and money than

---

[63]We have applied these criteria to PHMSA before when reviewing its gas integrity management program; see GAO-13-577.

building a new pipeline. Smaller-scale construction projects, such as short pipeline extensions, help meet the demands of shale areas like the Marcellus because the natural gas being produced is in close proximity to its destination market. Therefore, it is primarily a matter of connecting new gas production into the existing transmission pipeline network.

However, accommodating increased demand through new construction is a challenging proposition. To build a transmission pipeline requires a long-term commitment—often a contract that spans 30 to 50 years from producers. Major transmission pipeline projects may also face long timeframes. Pipeline companies we spoke with stated that once contracts are in place it usually takes 2 to 4 years to complete a pipeline. This is in part a result of the permitting process, which can include multiple federal and state agencies as well as obtaining rights to build on properties of individual land owners.[64] Timelines can be longer if the pipeline construction project is contentious.[65] The construction timeline is also dependent on terrain and weather. Pipeline industry representatives in West Virginia told us that constructing pipelines in mountainous terrains is much more difficult than in flat land. State officials in North Dakota said that long winters and short construction seasons cause construction projects to last over several construction seasons to complete. Other reasons provided by state officials and industry officials for a slower growth in pipeline infrastructure in North Dakota include the challenge of securing right-of-ways, as well as uncertainty in market demand. It is possible that continued shale exploration and development in other parts of the country could displace demand for Bakken shale products. Developers have proposed some future pipeline projects, and some have been approved in areas like North Dakota, but transmission pipeline mileage has not seen the same kind of rapid increase as gathering pipeline mileage. For example, Enbridge Energy Partners has proposed a transmission pipeline called Sandpiper that spans 612 miles from North Dakota through Minnesota to Wisconsin. The pipeline is proposed to be 24 inches and 30 inches in different places and will carry between

---

[64]GAO-13-221.

[65]For example, the Keystone pipeline, which would move approximately 100,000 barrels of Bakken crude oil per day, applied for a Presidential Permit in 2008, which has not been approved. For proposed petroleum pipelines that cross international borders of the United States, the President, through Executive Order (EO) 13337, directs the Secretary of State to decide whether a project serves the national interest before granting a Presidential Permit.

225,000 and 375,000 barrels of oil. WBI Energy announced planning for a 375-mile natural gas transmission line called the Dakota Pipeline in January 2014. The proposed route would start in North Dakota and continue into Minnesota.

In areas of shale development without access to an established pipeline network, such as the Bakken region, lengthy timelines and high costs associated with building transmission pipeline have led producers to seek alternative methods for transporting some of the production—primarily rail.

DOT Is Working to Address Risks Related to the Increase in Transportation of Oil by Rail

Crude Oil Is Transported Increasingly by Rail and Travels Long Distances in Large Volumes

The use of rail to transport crude oil from development areas to refineries has increased dramatically. STB data show that rail moved about 236,000 carloads of crude oil in 2012, which is 24 times more than the approximately 9,700 carloads moved in 2008 (see fig. 5).[66] Carloads further increased in 2013, with AAR reporting that Class I freight railroads originated 407,761 carloads of crude oil that year.[67]

---

[66]Due to a lag in data reporting, 2013 STB data were not available for this report.

[67]We did not independently verify the AAR data.

Figure 5: Estimated Number of Crude Oil Rail Carloads in the United States, 2008 to 2012

Estimated carloads per year (in thousands)

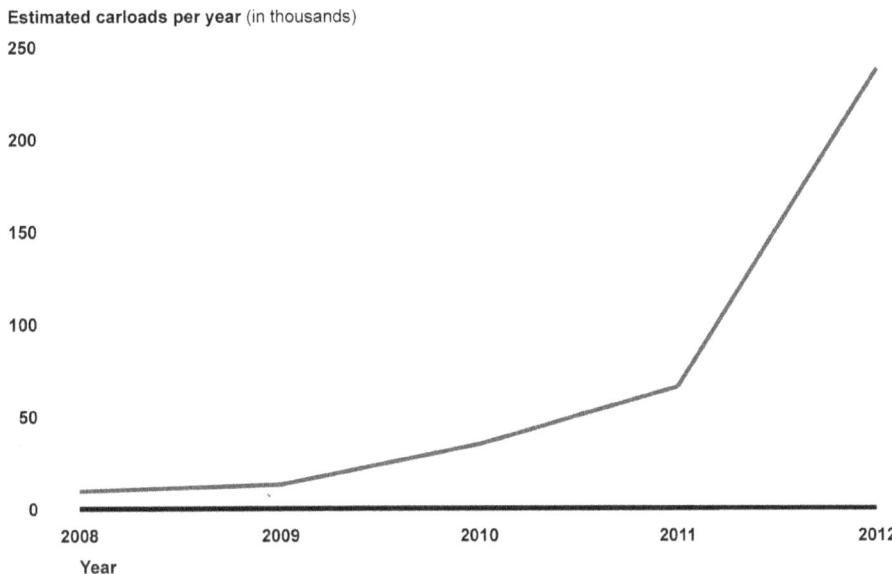

Year

Source: GAO analysis of Surface Transportation Board Data. | GAO-14-667

Note: The number of crude oil carloads, which was small in 2008-2011, had for those years a declining margin of error that started at 19 percent in 2008 and went down to about 8 percent in 2011. For 2012, the margin of error for crude oil carloads was less than 5 percent.

According to railroads, the majority of this increased movement of crude oil by rail is done using unit trains, which are trains that carry only one commodity to a single destination. Crude oil unit trains may consist of 80 to 120 tank cars, each carrying about 30,000 gallons of product, for a total of about 2.4 million to 3.6 million gallons of crude oil per train (see figure 6). This has resulted in an increase in demand for tank cars. According to AAR, nearly 50,000 tank cars were used to transport crude oil by rail as of April 2014.[68]

---

[68]Specifically, AAR stated that during the period of 2013 through April 2014, there were 104,597 tank cars used to transport flammable liquids by rail, including 49,182 tank cars used for crude oil.

GAO-14-667 Oil and Gas Transportation

Figure 6: Crude Oil Unit Train

There are different types of crude oil, which affects where crude is refined, as refineries are configured differently to handle the various types. This, in turn, affects where crude oil is transported for refining.[69] Increasingly, crude oil produced in the United States is "light and sweet" (lower in density and sulfur content); in contrast, a portion of new Canadian production has been "heavy and sour" crude oil (higher in density and sulfur content).[70] We have previously reported that not all U.S. refineries can take advantage of domestic crude oils to the same extent because of configuration constraints at some refineries.[71] Therefore, oil may travel long distances to a refinery with the matching refining configuration even if there is refinery capacity nearer to the crude oil source. According to an oil industry association in North Dakota, much of the domestic refining capacity for Bakken crude oil, which is a lighter crude, is located along the Gulf, East, and West Coasts. According to

---

[69]According to DOT officials, commodity price is also a factor in where crude oil is shipped.

[70]Crude oil is generally classified according to two parameters: density and sulfur content. Less dense crude oils are known as "light," while denser crude oils are known as "heavy." Crude oils with relatively low sulfur content are known as "sweet," while crude oils with higher sulfur content are known as "sour." In general, heavier and more sour crude oils require more complex and expensive refineries to process the crude oil into usable products.

[71]GAO-14-249.

STB data, about 69 percent of crude oil transported by rail in 2012 originated in North Dakota, followed by Texas and all other states (see fig. 7). STB data show that crude oil originating in North Dakota in 2012 traveled to 19 destination American states or Canadian provinces across North America. While most Bakken crude oil was shipped to destinations along the Gulf Coast, there was a large increase in oil shipped to East and West Coast destinations in 2012, signaling a shift in demand from the Gulf region to the other coasts.

Figure 7: North American Originations and Destinations of Crude Oil Carloads Hauled by Rail, 2012

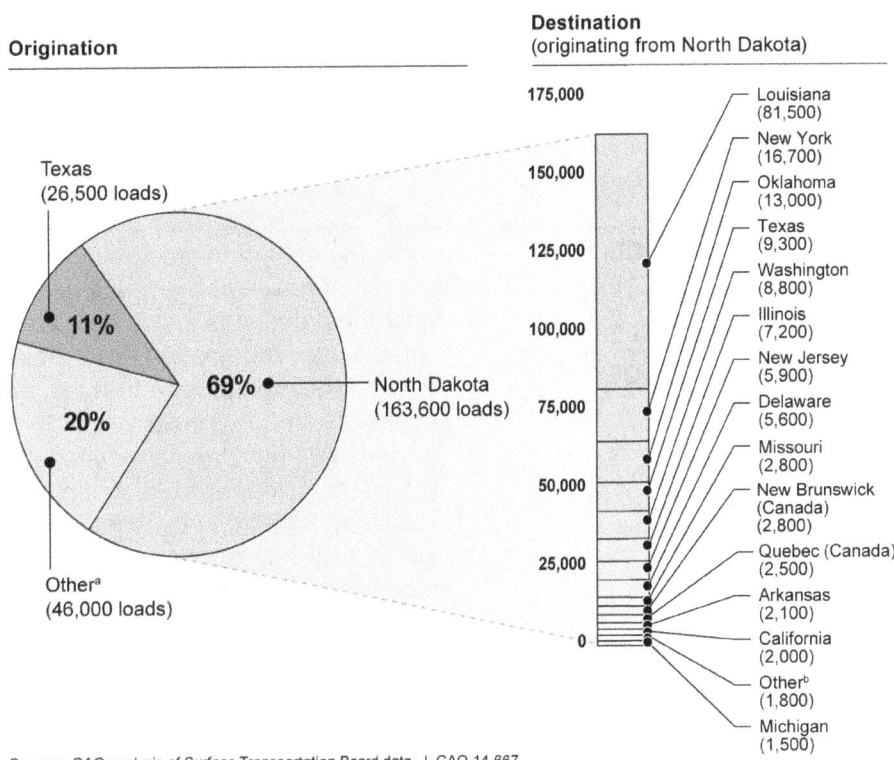

Sources: GAO analysis of Surface Transportation Board data. | GAO-14-667

[a]"Other" originations include 22 other American states and Canadian provinces, among the largest of which are Saskatchewan, Alberta, Oklahoma, California, and Colorado.

[b]"Other" destinations include 5 other American states and Canadian provinces where the estimated carloads received was fewer than 1,000, including oil that was shipped to final destinations within the state of North Dakota. Multiple destinations may exist in some states.

Notes: Carload numbers are rounded to the nearest hundred. The sum of carloads by destination does not equal the number of carloads originated in North Dakota due to rounding. The margins of error for estimates of carloads received by individual states or provinces are as follows: Missouri (57%), Quebec (55%), New Brunswick (52%), Arkansas (50%), California (40%), Delaware (40%), Michigan (38%), New Jersey (35%), Washington (32%), Texas (27%), Illinois (26%), Oklahoma (25%), New York (22%), and Louisiana (9%). For example, we are 95 percent confident that the value for Missouri is within +/- 57 percent of the estimate itself. Additionally, the relative margins of error for estimates of origination carloads are as follows: Texas (16%), North Dakota (7%), and all other originations (9%).

While pipelines generally deliver commodities to a fixed customer, rail offers the flexibility to serve different customers, allowing shippers to shift product quickly in response to market needs and price opportunities. Despite the great increase in crude oil transported by rail, the commodity remains a small percentage of railroads' business, comprising about 1.4 percent of Class I railroads' freight originations in 2013, according to AAR. As previously discussed, there are thousands of miles of track in the United States, providing various shipping opportunities for crude oil, as well as other commodities.[72] Officials from Class I railroads said they have not extensively added new infrastructure to specifically accommodate the increased shipping of crude oil by rail, although officials from some railroads said they have added track infrastructure in specific areas of increased shale oil development to increase capacity.

DOT Is Taking Action to Address Safety Risks Resulting from the Transport of Crude Oil by Rail

As the movement of crude oil by rail has increased, incidents, such as spills and fires involving crude oil trains have also increased. PHMSA's hazardous materials incident data show that rail crude oil incidents in the United States increased from 8 incidents in 2008 to 119 incidents in 2013.[73] These data show that the majority of the 2013 incidents were small; however, two incidents in 2013, in Aliceville, Alabama and Casselton, North Dakota resulted in large spills and greater damage. Significant incidents have continued to occur in 2014, including an April derailment and fire in Lynchburg, Virginia. During a presentation at an April 2014 forum on rail safety, NTSB noted that significant accidents involving crude oil have increased in recent years, with one incident occurring between 2008 and 2012 compared to eight incidents since 2012.

DOT, primarily through PHMSA and FRA, sometimes jointly, has taken steps to engage the rail and oil and gas shipping industries and emergency responders to address the safety of transporting crude oil by

---

[72]We have ongoing work examining freight congestion in railroad corridors and the impact on local communities.

[73]PHMSA's incident database can be searched at https://hazmatonline.phmsa.dot.gov/IncidentReportsSearch/ (accessed June 12, 2014).

rail, particularly in response to concerns stemming from the July 2013 Lac-Mégantic, Quebec accident:

- In August 2013, February 2014, and May 2014, DOT issued emergency orders to compel shippers and railroads to address safety risks by taking steps to secure unattended trains, ensure proper testing and packaging of crude oil, and notify emergency responders about crude oil shipments.[74] DOT also issued safety advisories during this period recommending additional actions.[75]

- In August 2013, PHMSA, with FRA assistance, initiated an ongoing special inspection program to examine whether crude oil rail shipments are appropriately tested and packaged. The effort consists of spot inspections, data collection, and testing crude oil samples taken from tank cars. Initial information from the program has identified deficiencies; DOT issued fines against three companies in February 2014 for not following proper crude oil packaging procedures. According to PHMSA officials, this effort inspects about 2 percent of Bakken crude oil trains.

- In September 2013, PHMSA issued an Advance Notice of Proposed Rulemaking seeking comments from industry and other stakeholders on improvements to standards for crude oil rail tank cars.[76] This action was in response to the railroad industry's 2011 petition for improved standards and recommendations from NTSB.

---

[74]FRA's August 2013 emergency order required railroads to take additional steps to secure unattended trains to prevent unintended movement; DOT's February 2014 emergency order, amended in March 2014, specified requirements for testing and classifying crude oil for transportation by rail and required shippers to package crude oil under the more stringent standards as allowed by regulation; DOT's May 2014 emergency order required railroads shipping 1,000,000 or more gallons of crude oil in a single train (about 35 car loads) to notify states' emergency response commissions about the movement of such trains through their states and which specific counties trains would be traveling through.

[75]DOT's August 2013 safety advisory recommended that railroads review the circumstances of the Lac-Mégantic accident and consider changes to their operating practices related to crew staffing, human factors, and train securement. DOT's November 2013 safety advisory reinforced the importance of proper testing and packaging for flammable liquids transported by train. DOT's May 2014 safety advisory asked companies to use tank cars with the highest integrity available for transporting Bakken crude oil and to avoid using older DOT-111 tank cars.

[76]78 Fed. Reg. 54849 (Sept. 6, 2013).

- In January 2014, PHMSA issued a safety alert notifying the general public, emergency responders, shippers, and carriers that Bakken crude oil may be more flammable than traditional heavy crude oil based on tests associated with PHMSA and FRA's special inspection program. PHMSA said it planned to issue final results of the tests at a later date.

- In February 2014, DOT entered into a voluntary agreement with AAR to improve the safety of moving crude oil by rail including increased track inspections, improved emergency braking capabilities, use of a risk-based routing tool to identifying the safest routes, travel at lower speeds, and emergency response training and planning.

- Also in February 2014, PHMSA officials met with emergency responders and industry groups to discuss training and awareness related to the transport of Bakken crude oil.

- In July 2014, DOT issued an update on PHMSA and FRA's joint special inspection program that includes results to date of their crude oil testing efforts and related discussion of the appropriate packaging of oil tested.

Additionally, in July 2014, PHMSA, in coordination with FRA, proposed new rules that align with key areas of concern cited by stakeholders: crude oil classification, testing, and packaging; crude oil tank car design; and emergency response. Specifically, PHMSA issued a Notice of Proposed Rulemaking seeking comment on proposals for new regulations to lessen the frequency and consequences of train accidents involving large volumes of flammable liquids, such as crude oil. The proposal includes new operational requirements for certain trains transporting a large volume of flammable liquids; revisions to requirements for crude oil classification, testing, and packaging; and improvements in tank car standards.[77] Additionally, PHMSA, also in consultation with FRA, issued an Advance Notice of Proposed Rulemaking seeking comments in response to questions about potential revisions to current regulations for emergency response planning for crude oil transported by rail.[78]

---

[77]79 Fed. Reg. 45016 (Aug. 1, 2014).

[78]79 Fed. Reg. 45079 (Aug. 1, 2014).

Crude Oil Classification, Testing, and Packaging

PHMSA's current regulations for transporting hazardous materials require that shippers classify and characterize the materials they ship to identify the materials' characteristic properties and select an appropriate shipping package based on those properties.[79] "Classification" refers to identifying a material's hazard class, which could be one or more from the list of nine in PHMSA's hazardous materials regulations, such as a flammable liquid or flammable gas. "Characterization" refers to ascertaining other characteristics of the product to determine its proper packing group, a designation based on risk that identifies acceptable packages.[80] Specifically, PHMSA's regulations classify crude oil as a flammable liquid and offer acceptable tank cars under three packing groups based on characteristics such as the oil's flash point—lowest temperature at which a liquid can vaporize to form an ignitable mixture in air—and boiling point.[81] PHMSA's regulations provide options for the tests shippers may use to determine these characteristics.[82] Crude oil with higher boiling and flash points is considered less risky, since it is less likely to form flammable vapor unless exposed to extreme temperatures, and more approved packaging choices exist for such oil than for oil with lower boiling and flash points that could form ignitable vapor at lower temperatures. Substances that are gases, rather than liquid, at ambient temperatures are even more flammable, and thus more stringent packaging requirements apply to flammable gases than to flammable

---

[79] 49 C.F.R. Parts 172 and 173.

[80] 49 C.F.R. § 172.101. Hazardous liquids, including crude oil, can be packaged under three sets of increasingly stringent requirements known as "packing groups," which range from the least restrictive group III to the most restrictive group I. In addition to specifying what types of tank cars may be used under each packing group, packing groups I and II require the shipper to develop a security plan that includes assessment of transportation security risks and measures to address those risks, see 49 C.F.R. § 172.800 (a)(6). According to PHMSA officials, the security plan would include planning for leaving a train unattended, which could have been a factor in the Lac-Mégantic accident, since that train was unattended at the time of the accident. The crude oil in the Lac-Mégantic accident had been assigned to packing group III, which does not require this plan. Subsequently, investigators have determined that it should have been assigned to packing group II, which would have required a plan. Details of the Lac-Mégantic accident are incomplete because the Transportation Safety Board of Canada's investigation of the accident is still ongoing. As of January 2014, the agency was completing its examination and analysis phase and planned to soon move onto its reporting phase.

[81] 49 C.F.R. § § 172.101(g), 173.120, 173.121, 173.242, 173.243, and 179.200.

[82] 49 C.F.R. § § 173.120(c) and 173.121 (a)(1).

liquids. In particular, flammable gases must be packaged in pressure tank cars, which provide additional safety in the event of an accident.[83]

According to PHMSA officials, because crude oil is a natural resource, it has greater characteristic variability than a hazardous material manufactured under strict specifications or quality guidelines. Thus, testing may need to be done more frequently to make sure the proper packaging rules are followed, since different rules may apply depending on the characteristics of a particular oil shipment. A review by Canadian transportation safety officials determined that the crude oil involved in the Lac-Mégantic accident was packaged under less stringent packing requirements than those which should have been followed, given the flammability characteristics of the oil involved. Although, as DOT officials pointed out, a different packing group would not have changed the package itself, since the type of tank car involved in the incident, the DOT-111 tank car, is allowed for crude oil transport under all three packing groups.[84]

Stakeholders we spoke to have differing views on the volatility of crude oil from the Bakken region, the area where the most crude oil is being shipped by rail. Some industry stakeholders, including the operators of Bakken crude oil rail terminals, characterized Bakken crude oil as being like any other crude oil produced in the United States, while other stakeholders said it has differences that may make it more volatile. In particular, PHMSA and AAR officials said that Bakken oil has variable composition and may sometimes contain higher than usual levels of dissolved natural gases. According to AAR officials, this can lead to flammable gases building up in a tank car during transport. AAR officials also said that the presence of natural gas makes fires more likely when crude oil tank cars are involved in an accident. Additionally, a May 2014 industry study noted that Bakken crude oil may contain higher amounts of dissolved flammable gases; however, the report states that it is not enough to warrant new regulations for crude oil rail transportation.[85]

---

[83]49 C.F.R § § 172.101, 173.115(a), 173.314, and 179.100.

[84]Transportation Safety Board of Canada, *Rail Safety Advisory Letter—12/13* (Gatineau, Quebec, Canada: Sept. 11, 2013).

[85]American Fuel & Petrochemical Manufacturers and Dangerous Goods Transport Consulting Inc., *A Survey of Bakken Crude Oil Characteristics Assembled For the U.S. Department of Transportation* (May 14, 2014).

According to PHMSA officials, the current regulatory framework for classifying and packaging crude oil for transport by rail may need to be further examined to ascertain if it addresses all of the risks posed by some shale crude oils that have properties unlike other typical crudes. PHMSA's July 2014 Notice of Proposed Rulemaking calls for shippers of mined gases and liquids to be transported by rail, including crude oil, to develop and implement a program for sampling and testing to ensure the shippers' materials are properly classified and characterized. The procedures must outline a frequency of sampling and testing that accounts for the potential variability of the material being tested, sampling at various points to understand the variability of the material during transportation, sampling methods that ensure a representative sample of the entire packaged mixture is collected, and testing methods used, among other requirements. The sampling and testing program must be documented in writing and retained for as long as it remains in effect and be made available to DOT for review upon request.

Representatives from railroads and crude oil terminals we spoke to, as well as from the oil and gas industry, have indicated that clarification about the requirements for testing and packaging crude oil is needed. Specifically, two of the railroads and two crude oil rail terminal operators told us that PHMSA needs to clarify its crude oil testing requirements, including to more clearly state which tests should be done and with what frequency.[86] One of the terminal operators told us that without clearer guidance, they are unsure whether they are performing the right tests and testing with sufficient frequency. They are also concerned they may be incurring unnecessary expense from over-testing. PHMSA's July 2014 Notice of Proposed Rulemaking does not state which tests should be performed or specifically how often, but does state that testing methods used should enable complete analysis, classification, and characterization of the material as required by PHMSA's regulations and that the frequency of testing should account for the potential variability of the material. The notice also seeks comment on whether more or less specificity of these requirements would aid shippers and whether the proposed guidelines provide sufficient clarity for shippers to understand whether they are in compliance. PHMSA has also drafted more detailed

---

[86]The other railroads did not mention the issue, and the third terminal operator said the current guidance is sufficient.

guidance on classification and packaging crude oil, including testing procedures, but had not released it publicly as of June 2014.[87]

Additionally, the American Petroleum Institute, an oil and gas industry association, formed a working group in 2014 to develop industry standards for testing and packaging of crude oil for transportation by rail, which the group hopes to implement by October 2014. PHMSA officials said that PHSMA scientists have been attending the group's meetings and providing input. In its July 2014 Notice of Proposed Rulemaking, PHMSA noted that it is encouraged by the development of an industry standard and that once finalized, PHMSA may consider adoption of such a standard.

Crude Oil Tank Car Design

Under PHMSA's current packaging regulations, a number of types of tank cars are approved for transporting crude oil.[88] However, DOT-111 tank cars are most commonly used, according to industry and railroad representatives, and PHMSA's regulations allow its use for all types of crude oil, regardless of packing group.

NTSB has documented a history of safety concerns with the DOT-111 tank car. Specifically, NTSB has raised concerns regarding the tank car's puncture resistance, heat tolerance, and potential for overpressurization during a fire. In its report of a 2011 investigation of the derailment of a train hauling ethanol tank cars, NTSB noted that its 1991 safety study and four train-derailment investigations from 1992 to 2009 had identified problems with DOT-111 tank cars.[89] The report further concluded that the car's poor performance suggested that DOT-111 tank cars are inadequately designed to prevent punctures and breaches and that the catastrophic release of hazardous materials can be expected when derailments involve DOT-111 cars.[90] In response to that and other rail incidents, in 2012, NTSB recommended that PHMSA upgrade its DOT-

---

[87]PHMSA provided us a draft of this guidance in March 2014; according to PHMSA officials, the document is still under development.

[88]49 C.F.R. § § 173.242(a) and 173.243(a),

[89]NTSB, *Railroad Accident Brief, NTSB/RAB-13/02* (Washington, D.C.: Aug.14, 2013).

[90]According to FRA officials, tank car specifications and design requirements were based on forces and stresses incident to normal transportation, not crash survivability, since derailments are not normal transportation events. Officials said that recently crash survivability has been a metric for tank car specification and design.

111 tank car standards to improve tank shielding and puncture resistance, a move the industry had already begun to address.

In 2011, the railroad industry petitioned PHMSA to adopt improved standards for DOT-111 tank cars and worked with tank car manufacturers and other stakeholders to develop improved industry standards that were implemented later that year. These standards called for a thicker shell to improve puncture resistance, shielding at both ends of the tank car, and protection for the top fittings of the tank car. More recently in November 2013, following the Lac-Mégantic accident, the railroad industry called for further tank car upgrades, including a thicker shell, protection to prevent overheating, additional shielding, protection for outlet handles on the bottom of a tank, and high-capacity pressure relief valves.[91] Figure 8 shows how these various proposed upgrades may be incorporated into a crude oil tank car.

---

[91]Additionally, an AAR official speaking at an NTSB forum and officials from one railroad that we spoke to suggested that the type of tank cars currently used may not be appropriate for transporting crude oil of higher flammability and that pressure tank cars may be preferable. PHMSA's hazardous materials regulations require flammable gases to be transported in pressure tank cars. According to FRA officials, if the vapor pressure of crude oil is high enough, regulations would require putting it in a pressure car. According to PHMSA's and FRA's July 2014 update on its special inspection effort, the current classification of Bakken crude oil as a flammable liquid is accurate under the current classification system; however, the update also notes that Bakken crude oil tested has a higher gas content, higher vapor pressure, lower flash point, and lower boiling point than most other crude oil in the United States. Consequently, the update concluded that Bakken crude oil has a higher degree of volatility than other oil, which correlates to increased ignitability and flammability.

Figure 8: Proposed Upgrades to Crude Oil Rail Tank Cars

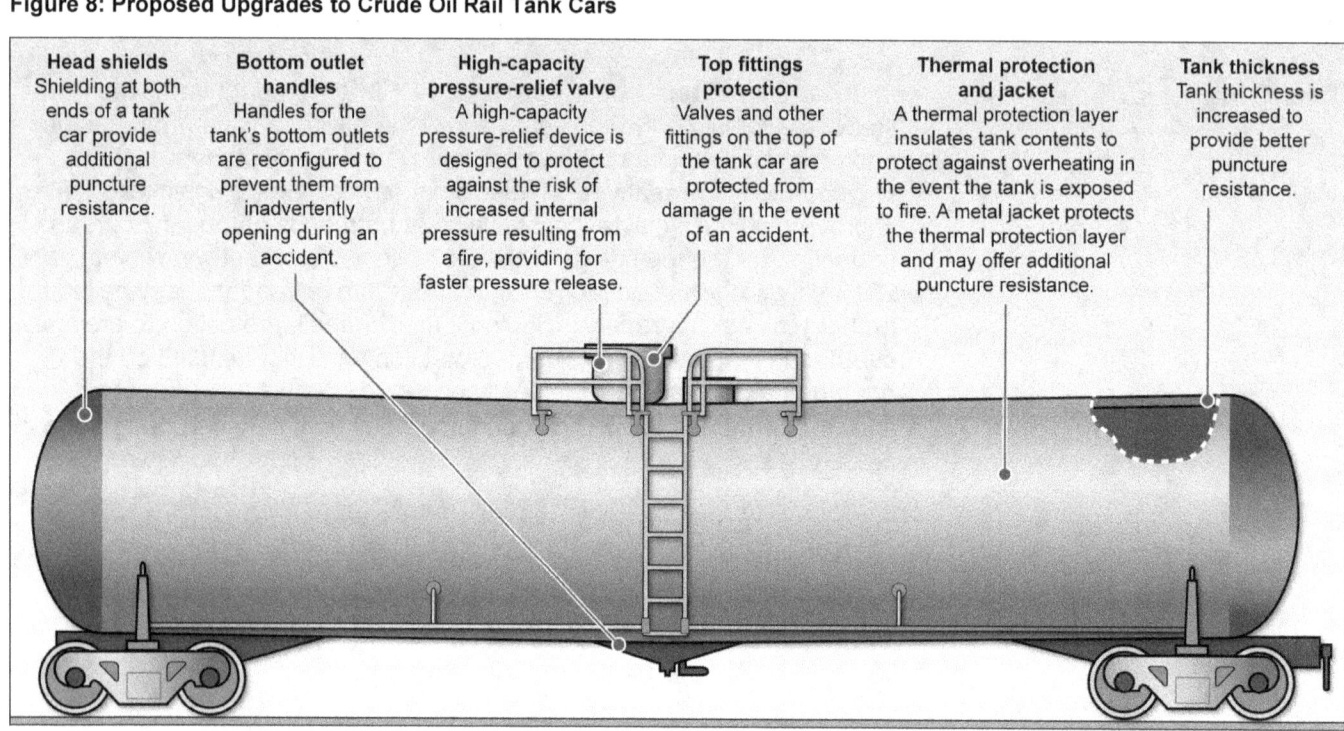

Head shields
Shielding at both ends of a tank car provide additional puncture resistance.

Bottom outlet handles
Handles for the tank's bottom outlets are reconfigured to prevent them from inadvertently opening during an accident.

High-capacity pressure-relief valve
A high-capacity pressure-relief device is designed to protect against the risk of increased internal pressure resulting from a fire, providing for faster pressure release.

Top fittings protection
Valves and other fittings on the top of the tank car are protected from damage in the event of an accident.

Thermal protection and jacket
A thermal protection layer insulates tank contents to protect against overheating in the event the tank is exposed to fire. A metal jacket protects the thermal protection layer and may offer additional puncture resistance.

Tank thickness
Tank thickness is increased to provide better puncture resistance.

Sources: GAO, AAR and railroads. | GAO-14-667

Although tank cars are generally owned by shippers or third parties, one railroad told us they intend to acquire their own fleet of tank cars built to the railroad industry's 2013 proposed standards. The railroad hopes to incentivize the cars' use by shippers; however, railroads are obligated to move materials as long as they are packaged according to federal standards, and told us they cannot force customers to use upgraded cars and have to accept cargo so long as it is in an allowable package, which includes older model DOT-111 cars.

A wide range of stakeholders we interviewed—including those from PHMSA, NTSB, state transportation agencies, railroad industry, and rail suppliers—told us that crude oil tank car standards need to be improved. Most shippers, railroads, and rail suppliers providing comments in response to PHMSA's September 2013 rail safety Advance Notice of Proposed Rulemaking also stated this opinion. However, there were some differences in their views on how improvements should be implemented. Those who commented in response to PHMSA's notice supported enacting the industry's upgraded tank car standard into regulation and were generally supportive of proposals to strengthen tank cars' puncture resistance through design features such as thicker tank walls, jackets, and shielding. However, stakeholders disagreed on the extent to which existing tank cars should—or even could—be retrofitted to meet higher standards. For example, shippers and rail suppliers stated that existing tank cars built to the current industry standards that already exceed the regulatory standard should be exempt from retrofitting if PHMSA were to adopt an even higher standard. Shippers also expressed concerns that retrofitting would be costly, take tank cars out of service, and put a burden on the already busy shops that also build new tank cars. Local-government and rail-industry commenters supported retrofitting existing cars.

In its July 2014 Notice of Proposed Rulemaking, PHMSA sought comment on requirements for a new DOT-117 tank car standard to replace the current DOT-111 standard for newly manufactured tank cars transporting flammable liquids, which could be one of three options: 1) a design by PHMSA and FRA that would increase puncture resistance, provide thermal protection, protect top fittings and bottom outlets, and improve braking performance; 2) the design in the railroad industry's proposal from November 2013 previously discussed; and 3) the 2011 industry-developed tank car design with some enhancements. PHMSA's Notice of Proposed Rulemaking concluded that cars built to the option 3 standard would likely be built in the absence of a new rule, based on commitments from industry, but that options 1 and 2 would provide additional safety benefits, along with additional cost. Specifically, PHMSA estimated that the improved braking, roll-over protection and increased shell thickness under option 1 would cost $5,000 more per car than option 3. According to PHMSA, option 2 would have most of the same safety features as option 1 except rollover protection and the improved braking system, resulting in a cost of $2,000 more per car than option 3. In addition to the new DOT-117 standard, the proposal would create a performance standard for the design and construction of new tank cars equivalent to the DOT-117, subject to FRA approval. Under the proposal, existing tank cars would have to be retrofitted to comply with the performance standard.[92] The proposal calls for phasing out use of all

---

[92] PHMSA's Notice of Proposed Rulemaking notes that retrofitting could be costly, potentially exceeding $30,000 per car, and would result in out-of-service time of at least 1 month. Due to cost concerns, PHMSA's proposal for retrofitting existing tank cars does not include requirements for top-fittings protections.

DOT-111 tank cars for transporting flammable liquids by October 1, 2020, although the cars could still be used to transport other materials.[93]

Although this proposed rule had previously been scheduled for release in November 2014, PHMSA accelerated its efforts to issue a proposal, resulting in the July 2014 release. According to PHMSA officials, the agency did not issue a proposal sooner because the industry, as well as the public, have had different opinions on tank car specifications. Since 2011, PHMSA has received multiple petitions seeking changes to tank car safety standards. In the interim, the railroad industry has moved to adopt higher standards, and in a May 2014 safety advisory, PHMSA and FRA asked companies to refrain from using older tank cars if possible.

Emergency Response

Transporting a large volume of flammable liquid in one train increases the risk of a large fire or explosion in the event of a derailment, such as in the Lac-Mégantic incident. DOT has noted that the transportation of crude oil in unit trains compounds the risk of ignition, and NTSB has reported that crude oil unit trains present the potential for disastrous consequences in the event of an accident. Associations representing emergency responders told us they are particularly concerned about the risk these trains pose to rural areas, which generally have fewer resources to respond to hazardous materials incidents. They also cited concerns with the general lack of awareness about risks and the need for industry to better communicate with local responders about them. Railroad officials told us that risks from unit trains can be managed. Further, railroad officials told us that transporting crude oil in trains that carry a mixture of freight commodities could be higher risk, due to the need to sort crude oil tank cars in rail yards, and that doing so would lead to reduced efficiency by increasing the turn-around times for crude oil trains. In August 2013, AAR revised its guidance on hazardous materials operating practices so that its restrictions would apply to crude oil unit trains; these restrictions include a 50 MPH speed limit, limitations on the use of track siding, and requirements for addressing defective bearings.[94] However, associations

---

[93]Specifically, PHMSA's Notice of Proposed Rulemaking states that existing DOT-111 tank cars may be retrofitted to DOT-117 standards, retired, repurposed, or operated under speed restrictions.

[94]AAR's hazardous materials operating practices guidance had previously applied to trains carrying poison inhalation hazards, toxic inhalation hazards, spent nuclear fuel, and high-level radioactive waste, but was expanded to also include trains carrying 20 car loads or intermodal portable tank loads of any combination of hazardous material, which would include unit trains carrying 20 or more carloads of crude oil.

representing emergency responders told us that industry should do more to prepare responders for potential incidents, such as by providing information, training, and resources. These organizations also shared concerns about rural responders lacking resources and information to respond as effectively as responders in urban areas. As previously mentioned, stakeholders told us that rural areas may lack sufficient resources to respond to a major event, like an accident involving a crude oil unit train.

As previously discussed, PHMSA has engaged emergency responders on crude oil transportation safety, and the voluntary commitment DOT secured from railroads included emergency response planning and training efforts. However, PHMSA's requirements for comprehensive emergency response planning do not apply to unit trains used to transport crude oil, raising concerns about the abilities of responders and other stakeholders to effectively handle potential incidents. As currently worded, PHMSA's regulations require comprehensive plans for trains that haul any liquid petroleum or non-petroleum oil in a quantity greater than 42,000 gallons per package—greater than the about 30,000 gallons of crude oil typically transported in a tank car—even though a unit train of 100 cars could carry about 3 million gallons of crude oil.[95] Instead, PHMSA requires railroads to have a basic plan that includes information about the maximum potential discharge, response plans, and identification of (but not coordination with) private response personnel and the appropriate people and agencies to contact in the event of an incident.[96] Federal regulations require that comprehensive emergency response plans include a written plan outlining contingency planning, an identified central coordinating official during an incident, private personnel secured by contract or other means to respond to a worst-case incident, training, equipment, and response actions and be subject to review by FRA.[97] Without a comprehensive plan, PHMSA does not have assurance that railroads have taken steps to plan for response needs and identified and coordinated with the appropriate responders. PHMSA's July 2014 Advance Notice of Proposed Rulemaking seeks comment on several

---

[95]The House Appropriations Committee called on PHMSA to address this problem in a report that accompanied the committee's Transportation-HUD appropriations bill H.R. 4745, for fiscal year 2015. H. Rpt. 113-464, p.62.

[96]49 C.F.R. § 130.31(a).

[97]49 C.F.R. § 130.31(b).

possible ways of expanding the comprehensive planning requirement to include crude oil unit trains by changing the threshold under which such plans are required.[98]

Although this review focuses on the packaging and movement of crude oil in tank cars, our prior work has found that while DOT has taken actions in this area, there are other safety issues that are also relevant to the context of the safety of transporting crude oil by rail. Specifically, in a December 2013 report, we found that FRA has developed a risk-based approach to direct its inspection efforts, but the agency had been slow to implement broader risk reduction planning.[99] As required by the Rail Safety Improvement Act of 2008, FRA was tasked with overseeing railroads' development of risk reduction plans.[100] Specifically, FRA was required to issue a final rule by October 2012 directing railroads to develop these plans, but our report found that FRA had not yet issued the final rule. Our report described safety challenges that railroads face, some of which can contribute to derailments. Other actions have been taken subsequently. FRA issued a final rule in January 2014 revising track inspection requirements to increase the standard for track used to transport hazardous materials.[101] And, as discussed, railroads entered into a voluntary agreement with DOT in February 2014 to improve the safety of crude oil trains.[102] In their comments in response to PHMSA's September 2013 Advance Notice of Proposed Rulemaking on rail safety, several shippers noted that recent incidents have generally been caused by defective track, railroad equipment or operational issues, and supported improvements in these areas. NTSB's accident report for the aforementioned 2011 derailment of ethanol tank cars noted that although problems with tank cars were a contributing factor, the probable cause of the accident was a broken rail. PHMSA has also noted that addressing

---

[98]Specifically, the notice asks whether the threshold should be set at 1) 1,000,000 gallons or more of crude oil per train, 2) 20 or more carloads of crude oil per train, 3) 42,000 gallons of crude oil per train, or 4) another threshold. The notice states that comments will inform a potential future Notice of Proposed Rulemaking on the issue.

[99]GAO, *Rail Safety: Improved Human Capital Planning Could Address Emerging Safety Oversight Challenges*, GAO-14-85 (Washington, D.C.: Dec. 9, 2013).

[100]Pub. L. No. 110-432, § 103, 122 Stat. 4848, 4853.

[101]79 Fed. Reg. 4234, 4245 (Jan. 24, 2014).

[102]Additionally, railroads we spoke to said they have invested heavily in upgrading their track in recent years.

the causes of derailments, not just upgrading tank cars, is important for improving the safety of transporting crude oil by rail. According to PHMSA officials, the severity of a derailment may present a wide range of forces for any particular tank car to withstand, and therefore, even an enhanced tank car may have variable performance and may not always perform better in a given derailment. PHMSA's July 2014 Notice of Proposed Rulemaking to address safety of transporting crude oil by rail includes a number of other provisions in addition to those already discussed for trains carrying 20 or more tank carloads of flammable liquids, including a routing analysis, enhanced braking, and codifying the May 2014 emergency order requiring notification to emergency responders about crude oil shipments.

Conclusions

The advent of new oil and gas production technologies has created a new energy boom for the United States. However, with this increase in production comes the responsibility to move those flammable, hazardous materials safely.

While the Department of Transportation has worked to identify and address risks, its regulation has not kept pace with the changing oil and gas transportation environment. Gathering pipeline construction has increased, but some of these new pipelines in rural areas fall outside the current safety framework, despite operating at the size and pressure (and therefore similar risk) as federally regulated transmission lines. DOT began a rulemaking to address this issue in 2011 but did not issue proposed rules. Subsequently, new gathering pipeline infrastructure has continued to grow, with industry predicting such growth will continue for the foreseeable future, raising concerns where such pipelines are not subject to safety regulations.

The growth in the use of rail to move crude oil has likewise revealed risks not fully addressed by the current safety framework, particularly in ensuring that oil is properly tested and packaged for shipping. Emergency responders also need to be adequately prepared in the event that incidents occur, both for pipeline and for rail. Recent transportation incidents, such as the July 2013 train accident in Lac-Mégantic, Quebec, have highlighted the need for risk-based federal safety oversight. Since the Lac-Mégantic accident, much emphasis has been placed on the need to upgrade standards for tank cars that carry crude oil, but attention to tank cars alone is not sufficient to address safety, a sentiment shared by some railroads and shippers, as well as DOT. Oil and gas shippers, railroads and pipeline operators, emergency responders, and government all have a role to play. Shippers, in particular, play an important role in making sure that hazardous materials like crude oil are properly packaged for safe transport. This underscores the importance of DOT's role in assessing the risk such oil poses and providing clear guidance for handling it safely. Without timely action to address safety risks posed by increased transport of oil and gas by pipeline and rail, additional accidents that could have been prevented or mitigated may endanger the public and call into question the readiness of transportation networks in the new oil and gas environment. DOT's recent proposed rulemakings to address concerns about transporting crude oil by rail signal the department's commitment to addressing these important safety issues. Because of the ongoing rail safety rulemakings, we are not making recommendations related to rail at this time.

Recommendation

To address the increased risk posed by new gathering pipeline construction in shale development areas, we recommend that the Secretary of Transportation, in conjunction with the Administrator of PHMSA, move forward with a Notice of Proposed Rulemaking to address gathering pipeline safety that addresses the risks of larger-diameter, higher-pressure gathering pipelines, including subjecting such pipelines to emergency response planning requirements that currently do not apply.

Agency Comments and Our Evaluation

We provided a draft of this report to DOT for comment. We received written comments from DOT's Assistant Secretary for Administration, which are reproduced in appendix III. These comments stated that PHMSA generally concurred with our recommendation to move forward with a rulemaking to address risks posed by gathering pipelines. Further, the letter stated that PHMSA is developing a rulemaking to revise its pipeline safety regulations and is examining the need to adopt safety requirements for gas gathering pipelines that are not currently subject to regulations. Additionally, the letter stated that proposed regulations are under development to ensure the safety of natural gas and hazardous liquid gathering pipelines that include collecting new information about gathering pipelines to better understand the risk they pose.

In the version of the draft report we sent to DOT for comment, we had also recommended that PHMSA develop and publish additional guidance on testing, classification and packaging of crude oil for transport by rail and that PHMSA address emergency response planning regulations for transporting oil by rail so that they include shipments of crude oil by unit trains. DOT's written response stated that PHMSA generally concurred with these recommendations and was taking steps to address them. Subsequently, on July 23, 2014, PHMSA, in coordination with FRA, issued rulemaking proposals that, if implemented, would likely address these concerns. Therefore, we are no longer making those recommendations in this report and we have added language to the report describing the objectives of the proposals. We also received technical comments from DOT, which we incorporated as appropriate.

As agreed with your offices, unless you publicly announce the contents of this report earlier, we plan no further distribution until 30 days from the report date. At that time, we will send copies of this report to the appropriate congressional committees and to the Secretary of Transportation. In addition, the report will be available at no charge on the GAO website at http://www.gao.gov.

If you or your staffs have any questions about this report, please contact Susan Fleming at (202) 512-2834 or flemings@gao.gov or Frank Rusco at (202) 512-3841 or ruscof@gao.gov. Contact points for our Offices of Congressional Relations and Public Affairs may be found on the last page of this report. Major contributors to this report are listed in appendix IV.

Susan Fleming
Director, Physical Infrastructure Issues

Frank Rusco
Director, Natural Resources and Environment

Appendix I: Objectives, Scope, and Methodology

This report addresses (1) challenges, if any, that increased domestic oil and gas production poses for U.S. transportation infrastructure and examples of associated risks and implications; (2) how pipeline infrastructure has changed as a result of increased oil and gas production, the key related safety risks, and to what extent the U.S. Department of Transportation (DOT) has addressed these risks; and (3) how rail infrastructure has changed as a result of increased oil production, the key related safety risks, and to what extent DOT has addressed these risks.

To identify challenges increased domestic oil and gas production poses for U.S. transportation infrastructure and examples of the associated risks and implications, we reviewed and synthesized information from 36 studies and other publications from federal, state, and tribal government agencies; industry; academics; and other organizations. We identified these studies and publications by conducting a search of web-based databases and resources—including Transport Research International Documentation, ProQuest, and FirstSearch—containing general academic articles, government resources, and "gray literature."[1] Studies and publications were limited to those focused on domestic onshore oil and gas production and published in the years 2008 through 2013. In addition, we reviewed prior work we have conducted. We included examples of known transportation infrastructure limitations and associated effects from these studies and publications in this report. We believe the studies and publications identified through our literature search and included in our review have identified key examples of known transportation infrastructure limitations and associated effects. In addition, we analyzed data from the U.S. Department of Energy's Energy Information Administration (EIA) to identify oil and gas produced from 2007 to 2012. To assess the reliability of these data, we examined EIA's published methodology for collecting this information and found the data sufficiently reliable for the purposes of this report.

---

[1]"Gray literature" publications may include, but are not limited to, the following types of materials: reports (pre-prints, preliminary progress and advanced reports, technical reports, statistical reports, memorandums, state-of-the art reports, market research reports, etc.), theses, conference proceedings, technical specifications and standards, non-commercial translations, bibliographies, technical and commercial documentation, and official documents not published commercially (primarily government reports and documents).

To determine how pipeline infrastructure has changed as a result of increased oil and gas production, we analyzed data from DOT's Pipeline and Hazardous Materials Safety Administration (PHMSA) on pipeline construction from January 1, 2010 through December 31, 2012 and interviewed PHMSA officials and representatives of pipeline industry associations and operators. We assessed the reliability of the data on pipeline construction by reviewing documentation about the database, interviewing agency officials about how the data are collected, comparing the data to similar information from EIA on completed pipeline projects, and reviewing the agency's related internal controls. We determined that the data were sufficiently reliable for describing new pipeline construction projects. We identified key pipeline safety risks by reviewing documents provided by and interviewing officials from PHMSA, pipeline industry associations and operators, and safety organizations. To examine trends in pipeline incidents, we analyzed PHMSA's pipeline incident data from January 1, 2008 through December 31, 2013. This analysis only examined transmission pipeline incidents, since many gathering pipelines are not regulated and therefore the data may not include potential gathering pipeline incidents. We assessed the reliability of these data by reviewing documentation on the collection of these data, interviewing agency officials about how the data are collected and whether there are potential limitations for using the data as we intended, and reviewing the agency's related internal controls. We determined that these data were sufficiently reliable for identifying trends in pipeline incidents. We also examined transportation infrastructure changes and safety risks specific to key shale development areas in four states selected because they are located above shale plays in different parts of the country with generally the highest levels of oil and gas production from 2007 through 2011, according to EIA data. The states and corresponding shale plays were Pennsylvania and West Virginia (Marcellus shale play), North Dakota (Bakken shale play), and Texas (Eagle Ford shale play). In these states, we spoke with state oil and gas regulatory and transportation agencies, oil and gas industry associations, oil and gas companies, railroads, and crude oil rail terminal operators, as well as a community advocacy organization in Pennsylvania. We also reviewed documents provided by these organizations.

To determine how rail infrastructure has changed, we analyzed Surface Transportation Board (STB) data on crude oil shipments by rail for calendar years 2008 through 2012 and interviewed DOT officials from

PHMSA and the Federal Railroad Administration and industry representatives, including railroads.[2] We assessed the reliability of the STB data by reviewing documentation about the data, interviewing agency officials about how the data were collected and ways they could be analyzed, and reviewing the agency's related internal controls. We determined that the data were sufficiently reliable for describing trends in the movement of crude oil. To identify the key safety risks related to changes in rail infrastructure, we analyzed PHMSA's data on rail hazardous-materials incidents from January 1, 2008 through December 31, 2013, reviewed documents submitted to a DOT rulemaking proceeding on rail safety, and interviewed DOT officials and representatives from safety organizations and industry. We assessed the reliability of PHMSA's incident data by reviewing documentation about the data, interviewing agencies officials about how the data were collected, testing the data for inconsistencies, and reviewing the agency's related internal controls. We concluded that the data were sufficiently reliable for discussing trends in rail hazardous-materials incidents. Additionally, to examine infrastructure impacts and safety issues closely associated with shale areas, we Interviewed officials from state oil and gas regulatory and transportation agencies, industry associations and oil and gas transportation companies in the four states mentioned previously: North Dakota, Pennsylvania, Texas, and West Virginia. To evaluate to what extent DOT has addressed safety risks, we reviewed federal laws and regulations, DOT emergency orders and guidance, and interviewed DOT officials. National and state-level stakeholders we interviewed are listed in tables 2 and 3.[3]

---

[2]In addition to DOT officials from PHMSA and FRA, we also interviewed officials from the Federal Highway Administration, Federal Motor Carriers Safety Administration, and Maritime Administration. Since we focused our evaluation of DOT's efforts on pipeline and rail, we did not evaluate the efforts of these other DOT administrations.

[3]Additionally, Kinder-Morgan, an oil pipeline operator, declined to participate, and Enbridge, an oil pipeline company, was not able to schedule an interview with us within our time frame. We also contacted five other crude oil rail terminals in North Dakota that either did not respond to our requests or declined to be interviewed.

Table 4: National-Level Industry and Safety Stakeholders GAO Interviewed

Stakeholder	Description
Industry stakeholders	
American Petroleum Institute	Oil and gas industry
American Short Line and Regional Railroad Association	Railroad industry
American Trucking Associations	Trucking industry
Association of American Railroads	Railroad industry
Association of Oil Pipe Lines	Pipeline industry
BNSF Railway	Class I railroad
CN	Class I railroad
Canadian Pacific	Class I railroad
CSX Transportation	Class I railroad
Dominion	Gas pipeline operator
Interstate Natural Gas Association of America	Pipeline industry
National Tank Truck Carriers	Trucking industry
Norfolk Southern	Class I railroad
Railway Supply Institute	Tank car manufacturers
Spectra	Gas pipeline operator
Williams/Transco	Gas pipeline operator
Union Pacific Railroad	Class I railroad
Safety stakeholders	
Commercial Vehicle Safety Alliance	Highway safety
International Association of Fire Chiefs	Emergency responders
National Association of Regulatory Utility Commissioners	State regulatory officials
National Association of State Fire Marshals	Emergency responders
National Fire Protection Association	Emergency responders
National Transportation Safety Board	Federal incident investigation
Pipeline Safety Trust	Pipeline safety advocates

Source: GAO. | GAO-14-667

Table 3: State-Level Stakeholders GAO Interviewed

Stakeholder	Description
North Dakota	
Crestwood Colt Hub	Rail crude oil terminal operator
Hess Corporation	Rail crude oil terminal operator
North Dakota Department of Mineral Resources	State oil and gas regulator
North Dakota Department of Transportation	State highway agency
North Dakota Petroleum Council	Oil and gas industry
North Dakota Pipeline Authority	State pipeline agency
North Dakota Pipeline Association	Pipeline industry
North Dakota Public Service Commission	State oil and gas regulator
Savage Services	Rail crude oil terminal operator
Pennsylvania	
C.O.G.E.N.T.	Community pipeline safety
MarkWest	Gas company
Pennsylvania Department of Transportation	State transportation agency
Pennsylvania Public Utility Commission (Gas Safety Division)	State gas regulator
Wheeling & Lake Erie Railroad	Regional railroad
Texas	
Gardendale Railroad	Short line railroad
Marathon Oil	Oil and gas pipeline operator
Railroad Commission of Texas	State oil and gas regulator
South Texas Energy Economics Roundtable	Oil and gas industry
Southcross	Gas company
Texas Department of Transportation (Rail Division)	State rail agency
Texas Oil and Gas Association	Oil and gas industry
Texas Pipeline Association	Pipeline industry
West Virginia	
Energy Partners	Gas pipeline operator
West Virginia Department of Transportation (Division of Highways)	State highway agency
West Virginia Public Safety Commission	State oil and gas pipeline regulator

Source: GAO. | GAO-14-667

We conducted this performance audit from August 2013 to August 2014 in accordance with generally accepted government auditing standards. Those standards require that we plan and perform the audit to obtain sufficient, appropriate evidence to provide a reasonable basis for our findings and conclusions based on our audit objectives. We believe that

the evidence obtained provides a reasonable basis for our findings and
conclusions based on our audit objectives.

Appendix II: Impacts of Shale Oil and Gas Development on Highways in Selected States

Pipeline and rail are used to transport shale oil and gas long distances; however, truck transportation via local roads and highways also plays an important role. Trucks transport these goods from production areas to pipeline and rail as well as haul most materials needed to develop oil and gas, such as water, sand, and equipment used during drilling and hydraulic fracturing. State agencies within the four states we examined (Pennsylvania, North Dakota, Pennsylvania, and Texas) have noted significant local road and highway impacts and safety concerns as a result of shale oil and gas development and have taken steps to address these impacts.

Infrastructure Impacts

States have reported a significant increase in truck traffic as a result of shale oil and gas development, the effects of which are particularly acute in rural areas unused to this level of road congestion. State officials provided estimates of the number of truck-loads required to drill and fracture a shale gas well ranging from about 1,200 to about 3,000. Although the number of trucks is greatest during the initial drilling and fracturing phases, significant truck volume may return if a well is re-fractured and, in the case of oil wells, trucks can be used to remove oil if the wells are not connected by pipeline. State officials told us that roads in many of these areas prior to development were built for light local and farm use and were not built for the additional thousands of heavy truck loads associated with oil and gas development, leading to deterioration. North Dakota officials told us that many of the roads the oil industry is using were built to handle approximately 600 loads a day and now these roads can see thousands of heavy truck loads per day. Officials also told us that state-wide, truck traffic accounts for approximately 18 percent of all traffic, but in development areas truck traffic can account for 35 to 50 percent. As a result, it has been much more difficult to predict where the biggest road deterioration is going to happen because it depends on the location and intensity of shale development. In Pennsylvania, officials told us the increased volume of trucks has shortened the roads' normal life cycle, leading to accelerated deterioration and significant damage. The costs of shoring up and rebuilding roads to address these impacts are significant. The Texas Department of Transportation estimated an annual impact to farm-to-market roads, state highways, and local roads in the Eagle Ford area of about $4 billion.

Safety Concerns

Road deterioration and increased truck volumes have created safety concerns in these states. Reported highway incidents involving crude oil have increased in recent years in North Dakota and Texas, the two states we examined with significant shale oil development.[1] In Texas, for example, the Texas Department of Transportation reported an increase in highway crashes in the Eagle Ford shale and Permian Basin areas, with the Permian area seeing a 13 percent increase in roadway fatalities between 2012 and 2013.

Actions to Address Impacts and Safety

The following actions are examples of ways state officials said they have addressed highway infrastructure and safety concerns:

- *Extraction taxes.* Officials in North Dakota told us the state uses taxes on extracted mineral resources to pay for road improvements. In 2013, the Texas state legislature voted to transfer a portion of the state's oil and gas severance tax to pay for road maintenance, a measure that will go before Texas voters for approval in November 2014.

- *Use agreements.* In Pennsylvania and West Virginia, states have entered into road-use agreements with energy companies making the companies responsible for their damage to the roads and maintaining them. Companies must also pay a bond as part of the agreement. Officials told us these agreements have helped make companies more responsible for their impact. For example, in Pennsylvania, officials told us industry had invested over $750 million in roadway infrastructure improvements.

- *Public awareness.* Texas launched a public education campaign to alert drivers to the need to use caution when driving through energy-related work zones.

Although much of the impact has been on rural, nonfederal roads, the Federal Highway Administration has been involved in helping states to coordinate information sharing. For example, in 2011, the Federal Highway Administration hosted an information-sharing meeting between officials in Pennsylvania and West Virginia, who told us the session was beneficial.

---

[1]The other two states, Pennsylvania and West Virginia, have shale formations where natural gas is primarily developed, which is not transported by truck.

Appendix III: Comments from Department of Transportation

U.S. Department of
Transportation

Office of the Secretary
of Transportation

1200 New Jersey Ave., SE
Washington, DC 20590

Ms. Susan Fleming
Director, Physical Infrastructure
U.S. Government Accountability Office
441 G Street NW
Washington, DC 20548

Re: GAO Draft Report on Oil and Gas Transportation (GAO-14-667)

Safety is the Department's top priority. Over the past 12 months, the Department has aggressively increased its efforts to improve the safe transport of crude oil and other hazardous materials through emergency orders, voluntary agreements with the industry, and regulatory actions.

The Department combined immediate actions to protect safety with a comprehensive longer term approach to address the transportation safety challenges related to new domestic energy production. The Pipeline and Hazardous Materials Safety Administration (PHMSA) and the Federal Railroad Administration (FRA) are working on comprehensive long term solutions to the issues concerning crude oil transportation by rail and have also made full and appropriate use of regulatory authority including Emergency Orders and enhanced oversight to address urgent public safety issues.[1] The Department has taken numerous specific actions to date, including:

- **Safety Alerts and Advisories** – have been issued warning of potential safety challenges and calling for the proper classification and management of crude shipments and the use of enhanced tank cars.
- **Emergency Orders (EO)** – requiring companies to address the risks associated with rail transportation of crude oil, including proper testing and classification, and notification requirements to ensure State Emergency Response Commissions are aware of shipments.
- **Enhanced Oversight** - to verify industry actions have resulted in enforcement action including three Notices of Probable Violations.
- **Voluntary Measures** – were enacted through agreements with industry to implement a number of voluntary measures that immediately improved safety.
- **Updated Regulations** –
  - The Department announced a comprehensive Notice of Proposed Rulemaking (NPRM), on July 23, 2014. This proposed rule would strengthen tank car standards for new and existing tank cars used to transport ethanol and crude oil. The proposed rule would also require offerors of mined gases and liquids to create a sampling and testing program to aid in proper classification and impose operational restrictions on railroads that transport large volumes of these liquids, including speed restrictions and advanced braking systems.

---

[1] For more details of the actions taken to date, please visit our Safe Delivery website at:
http://phmsa.dot.gov/hazmat/osd/calltoaction

2

- ○ The Department also announced an Advanced Notice of Proposed Rulemaking (ANPRM), on July 23, 2014, which requests comment on revisions to the thresholds requiring a comprehensive Oil Spill Response Plans (OSRP), clarity of the current comprehensive OSRP plan requirements, and costs of developing and implementing comprehensive OSRP.
  - ○ Additionally, proposed regulations are under development to ensure the safety of natural gas and hazardous liquid gathering lines that include collecting new information about gathering lines to better understand the risks they pose.
- **Encouraging States** – to adopt requirements that go beyond Federal Regulations for gathering lines. Both the federal government and the states have jurisdiction over gathering pipelines.
- **Workshops** – have been conducted to engage industry on technical and safety topics related to the safe transport of crude by pipeline and gathering lines.
- **National Standards Committee** – PHMSA actively participates in national consensus standards incorporated by reference in pipeline safety regulations.

The Department will continue to develop long term comprehensive solutions including new technologies, constructive interaction with industry, and effective oversight to mitigate risk and enhance safety through all phases of oil and gas transport.

PHMSA generally concurs with the recommendation concerning gathering line safety and is developing a rulemaking to revise the Pipeline Safety Regulations applicable to gas transmission and gathering pipelines, and examining the need to adopt safety requirements for those gas gathering lines that are not currently subject to the regulations. PHMSA also generally concurs with the recommendation for additional guidance for testing, classification and packaging of crude oil transport by rail, and is considering alternatives for providing that information (e.g., revised regulation or industry guidance). PHMSA also generally concurs with the recommendation related to emergency response planning, and will ensure that the public is afforded the opportunity to comment on appropriate regulatory thresholds. The Department will provide a detailed response to each recommendation within 60 days of the GAO report issuance.

We appreciate the opportunity to offer additional perspective on the draft report. Please contact Martin Gertel, Director of Audit Relations, at 202-366-5145 with any questions or if you would like to obtain additional detail about these comments.

Sincerely,

Brodi Fontenot
Assistant Secretary for Administration

Appendix IV: GAO Contacts and Staff Acknowledgments

GAO Contacts	Susan Fleming, (202) 512-2834 or flemings@gao.gov
	Frank Rusco, (202) 512-3841 or ruscof@gao.gov

Staff Acknowledgments	In addition to the individuals named above, Karla Springer (Assistant Director), Sara Vermillion (Assistant Director), Melissa Bodeau, Lorraine Ettaro, Quindi Franco, David Hooper, Andrew Huddleston, John Mingus, Joshua Ormond, James Russell, Holly Sasso, Jay Spaan, Jack Wang, Amy Ward-Meier, and Jade Winfree made key contributions to this report.